852258

MAR 5 1992

Questions of Today

TERRORISTS
OR FREEDOM FIGHTERS?

Charles Freeman

B.T. Batsford Ltd, London

Contents

1 The terrorist attack 3

2 What is terrorism? 6

3 Case Study: Terrorism in Northern Ireland 20

4 Case Study: The Palestinians and Israel 30

5 Terrorism: strategies and effects 41

6 The fight against terrorism 48

7 Terrorism: a conclusion 58

Suggestions for further reading 61

Glossary 62

Index 64

© Charles Freeman 1990
First published 1990

All rights reserved. No part of this publication may be reproduced in any form or by any means,
without permission from the Publisher.

Typeset by Tek-Art Ltd Kent
and printed and bound
in Great Britain by
The Bath Press, Bath
for the publishers
B.T. Batsford Ltd
4 Fitzhardinge Street
London W1H 0AH

ISBN 0 7134 6076 8

Cover illustration: *Terrorist or freedom fighter? A Palestinian with his weapon.*

Acknowledgments

The Author and Publishers would like to thank the following for kind permission to reproduce illustrations in this book: Associated Press for pages 35, 39, 45, 50; Camera Press for pages 10, 11, 18, 22, 23, 31, 34, 49a, 49b, 51a, 51b; The Hulton Picture Company for pages 16a, 32, 37; I.D.A.F. for page 7; The Keystone Collection for pages 12a, 17, 24, 26, 33 and 42; Magnum Photos for page 12b; The Press Association for pages 5, 46; Frank Spooner Pictures for page 38.

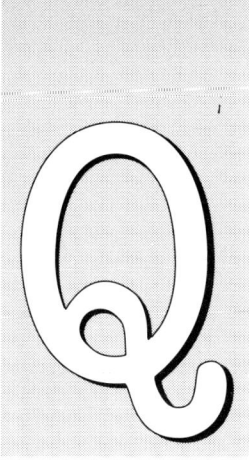

1 The terrorist attack

On 5 April 1988, an airliner from Kuwait, a small oil-rich state at the northern end of the Persian Gulf, was on its way from Thailand home to Kuwait. There were 97 passengers and 15 crew on board.

Suddenly a group of hijackers appeared from among the passengers. They seized control and ordered the pilot to change direction and fly to Iran. The plane eventually landed at Mashhad, a city in the northwest of Iran.

The hijackers then announced their demands. Seventeen prisoners held by the government of Kuwait must be released. If they were not, the lives of all the passengers, but especially those from Kuwait, would be at risk.

Who were these prisoners and who were the hijackers?

In December 1983 a number of explosions had rocked Kuwait City. Eventually a number of the bombers, 17 of them in all, had been arrested by the Kuwaiti government and sentenced to imprisonment. It appeared that they were members of a group calling themselves Al Jihad al-Islami (Arabic for Islamic Holy War). Al Jihad al-Islami was based in the Lebanon but had strong links with the Iranian government. The Iranians were, it seemed, using the group to launch the bomb attacks against Kuwait because Kuwait had been supporting the Iraqi government in its war with Iran.

Now it looked as if Al Jihad was launching another attack, this time a hijacking, to get the bombers released.

During 6 and 7 April, 66 passengers were released by the hijackers. Most of those left were Kuwaitis but the Kuwaiti government firmly refused to release the bombers. On 8 April, the Iranians allowed the plane to be refuelled. It set off westwards towards the Lebanon, where the hijackers were hoping to land at Beirut Airport. However, they were refused permission to land and with fuel running low, the pilot pleaded successfully to be allowed to land at Larnaca Airport in Cyprus.

The hijackers now decided to increase the pressure on the Kuwaiti government. On 9 April they shot one of the passengers and threw his body out onto the tarmac. On 11 April another was shot. As the tension mounted, the Kuwaiti government still stood firm and the Cyprus government refused to refuel the plane.

Meanwhile direct contact was kept with the hijackers through the control tower of the airport. It became clear that they were a tough and determined group who would not give in easily. There seemed to be deadlock.

The days passed. Finally, on 12 April a deal was made. Twelve passengers were released (leaving 34 passengers and crew on the plane). Then the plane was refuelled. It would be allowed to fly on to Algeria where the passengers would all be released and the hijackers allowed to go free.

On 13 April the plane set off for Algeria. When it landed, however, the hijackers seemed to go back on their deal. They told pressmen that the plane would be blown up if the Kuwaiti government did not give in. Another week went by. Finally, 20 April, 15 days after the hijack had begun, the passengers and crew were suddenly

THE TERRORIST ATTACK

End of a hijack. The Kuwaiti airliner at Algiers airport before the release of the hostages.

released. The hijackers had, apparently, already been allowed to escape and reports suggested that they had been flown back to the Lebanon. The hijack was over but the hijackers had escaped unpunished.

This was an act of international terrorism. A group of innocent people, the passengers and crew of the aircraft, had been seized and subjected to a terrifying ordeal which for many of them lasted for 15 days and for two of them ended in death.

Such acts of terrorism raise many issues, some of which will be discussed later in this book. Why had it proved so easy to seize the aircraft? Who exactly had planned, paid for and carried out the attack? How should such hijackings be handled? How far should governments be prepared to negotiate or give in to terrorists' demands in order to save lives? Who should deal with the hijackers if captured and what sort of penalties should be inflicted on them?

ENNISKILLEN, NORTHERN IRELAND. REMEMBRANCE DAY, 8 NOVEMBER 1987

'At eleven o'clock we should have been remembering the dead. Instead we were pulling them out.' (*Enniskillen teenager quoted in a newspaper report.*)

8 November 1987 was Remembrance Day throughout Britain, the day in which the nation gathered around its war memorials to remember those who had died in the wars of the twentieth century. Enniskillen,

THE TERRORIST ATTACK

a small Protestant town in Northern Ireland, was no different in this respect from many towns on mainland Britain. Crowds were gathering, processions of children, bands, soldiers and policemen were getting ready to march towards the memorial to lay their wreaths.

Many of the onlookers had lined up against a Catholic social club, St Michael's Reading Rooms. Suddenly, at 10.45 a.m. a quarter of an hour before the memorial service was to begin, there was a shattering explosion from within the hall. The walls were blown out and the end wall fell over the spectators. Survivors dug desperately to free those covered by the rubble. They were too late for many. Eleven were dead. Sixty-three more were injured.

Most of the dead were elderly, seven of them over 60. One was a retired policeman, another an off-duty policeman. The rest were all civilians. The youngest victim was Marie Wilson, aged 20. Like all the others she was a Protestant but she was training to be a nurse at the Royal Victoria Hospital in Belfast, which served a largely Catholic area of the city. Among the injured were 13 children, one of them a baby only two months old.

At first no one claimed responsibility for the bomb. At last, 30 hours later, the Provisional IRA admitted they were responsible. They claimed that the bomb had been aimed at soldiers who would be patrolling the area and had been triggered off not by the IRA but by British army signalling devices. No evidence was ever found that the army had triggered it off. Meanwhile, another IRA bomb was found in Tullyhommon 30 miles from Enniskillen. It failed to explode.

This act of terrorism was very different from the Kuwaiti hijacking. Here the bombers came from within the community. It was a single swift act of violence compared with the long drawn out agony of the hijacking. Despite the differences, it marked another example of the power of the terrorist in today's world.

The funeral procession of retired policeman Sam Gault passes the site of the Enniskillen Remembrance Day bombings and Enniskillen war memorial, November 1987.

2 What is terrorism?

Probably the first image that comes into our minds when we hear the word terrorism is violence. Terrorism is the bomb that explodes in a crowded street, the man gunned down on his doorstep in front of his family, the aircraft that is seized by armed hijackers.

This violence often seems to involve innocent people, the bystanders at Enniskillen waiting for a service to begin, the passengers of many different nationalities who happen to be travelling on the same aircraft. Terrorist violence has often been described as indiscriminate: that is, its victims are picked at random. This is not always the case. Often terrorists will target particular people, leaders of a community, the police or members of the armed forces. However, even in these cases there is the sudden and unexpected act of violence, the horror of a human being gunned down or bombed by self-appointed assassins.

What are terrorists trying to do with these acts of sudden violence? In most cases they are aiming to spread fear. Terrorists, one observer has said, do not care about whom they kill, but who is **frightened** by their killing. Terrorists are trying to put pressure on a community through the use of violence, in order to force that community to agree to their demands. In Chapter Three we shall look in more detail at why terrorists believe the spread of fear will help their cause. Meanwhile, as far as this book is concerned, *terrorism can be seen as the use of fear, through violence or the threat of violence, as a weapon to force political change.* Fundamental to the spread of fear is the effective use of publicity and the more brutal or daring the act of terrorism, the more effective the international publicity for the terrorists.

In much of this book we shall be looking at small groups who are using terrorism to overthrow governments or to force them to change their policies. It is important to note, however, that governments themselves can use terrorism as a means of achieving *their* ends; the suppression of opponents, for example. The use of fear in this way is of particular concern, as governments have enormous resources at their disposal – the police and the armed forces – as well as the control of publicity. The use of terrorism by governments – or state terrorism – is discussed opposite.

WHY HAS TERRORISM BECOME SUCH A MAJOR ISSUE IN THE PAST 20 YEARS?
The use of terrorism as a weapon is not new. We can find examples throughout history, although the word itself was probably used for the first time in the 1790s to describe the Reign of Terror of the French Revolution. However, in the past 20 years, terrorism as a political weapon has been given greater prominence than ever before. What are the reasons for this?

We need first to look at the nature of the world we live in. The twentieth century has been an era of violence. There have been two massive world wars and scores of other conflicts, many of them bringing appalling local destruction. Violence has become, in many different situations, a common way of trying to achieve change. It is not surprising that its use has become accepted as justified by many groups and individuals, who feel they have a good

WHAT IS TERRORISM?

The power of the state, here in South Africa. States with the determination to do so, can easily terrorize their inhabitants.

FOCUS ON . . . .

Terrrorism by the state

'The normal attitude of the torturers and guards towards us was to consider us less than slaves. We were objects and rather troublesome objects at that. They would say, "You're dirt. Since you disappeared, you're nothing. Anyway, nobody remembers you. You don't exist. We are everything for you. We are justice. We are God." '

These are the words of an imprisoned victim of the military government of General Galtieri of Argentina (1976-83). They remind us of the power a state can use to crush its opponents. While in most of this book we will be discussing the use of terrorism by small groups, governments or states (if we use the word to describe the apparatus of government, its civil servants, police, army and judges) are just as able to use terrorism against their opponents. Any campaign in which widespread killing, torture or imprisonment by government forces takes place without effective restraint can be seen as one of terrorism. Victims are killed or tortured not just to silence them but to frighten others into submission.

The use of terrorism by states has become an all too common feature of the second half of the twentieth century. The state has enormous power at its command and there is normally no other organized group in the land which can successfully resist it. This is, of course, one of the main differences between state terrorism and other forms. **State terrorism is not a weapon of the weak against the strong but of the strong against the weak**.

Secondly, as we shall see, a major part of modern terrorism by small groups is the search for publicity. The terrorist is using violence to shock and achieve headlines. Much state terrorism is concealed within the prison and torture chamber. It may be concerned with frightening the local community, but not with bringing fear to the world at large.

WHAT IS TERRORISM?

cause. In a troubled world, with extremes of wealth and poverty and many racial and nationalist conflicts, there is certainly no shortage of such causes.

These developments, although important, do not fully explain why terrorism has become so widespread.

One reason lies in the publicity that terrorism brings. A bombing, shooting or hijacking can be transmitted from one end of the world to another in minutes. Television screens bring the horror and drama of many terrorist acts right into our living rooms.

It is this very development which has been exploited by terrorists. The terrorist knows the greater the publicity an act of terrorism achieves, the greater the fear and anxiety that is spread. To this extent, terrorism and the news media feed on each other and make the impact of terrorism all the greater.

Another important development in terrorism has been in the mobility of terrorists. The hijacking of the Kuwaiti aircraft is an excellent example of this. No less than six different governments across half the world were involved in the events of these 15 days. The international nature of terrorism, the way in which groups can build links with each other or with groups that support them – and then strike in virtually any part of the world – has given terrorism a totally new dimension in the past 20 years. We call acts of terrorism of this nature **international terrorism**. International terrorism has been made more dangerous in recent years by the support certain governments, particularly in the Middle East, have given to terrorist groups (see the example of Gadhaffi, page 36).

At the same time the weapons of terrorism have become more sophisticated. The destructive power of guns has increased dramatically. An easily concealed machine gun can kill and wound tens of people in a few minutes (as happened in the Lod Airport massacre of 1972 in Israel, when 26 people were killed and 80 wounded in a few seconds by three

---

FOCUS ON....

Semtex

'The most dangerous weapon used by the IRA', one British army expert is reported to have said, 'is not SAM missiles but Semtex.'

Semtex is a plastic explosive, made since the end of the 1960s in Czechoslovakia. There is no evidence that Czechoslovakia has supplied Semtex directly to terrorist groups but many governments throughout the world have bought it and some of these have passed it on to terrorists. One major source has been Libya, which has supplied the IRA with enough Semtex to last it for years.

Semtex is an ideal weapon for terrorists. It has no smell and cannot be detected by X-rays. Unlike other explosives such as gelignite, it appears to stay active for years. It can be moulded into different shapes to fit any space which the terrorist chooses. The IRA, for instance, packs amounts as little as 2lbs into lunch boxes and then attaches these under cars. By the end of 1988 about a dozen people had been killed in this way.

A major use of Semtex has been to blow up planes. Middle East groups have specialized in this. Because it is so difficult to detect it is relatively easy to smuggle aboard. Only a few pounds of carefully placed Semtex are needed to blow a hole in an aircraft, causing it to disintegrate in mid-air. The Lockerbie air disaster of December 1988 was caused by explosives similar to Semtex.

Semtex will continue to be a major terrorist weapon until some effective method of detecting it is found. One plan is to ensure that the makers of Semtex mix in special microchips which could then be spotted. However, there is so much pure Semtex already freely available it is unlikely this would prove effective for many years. There are also other plastic explosives available, and the manufacture of all these would have to be controlled.

gunmen). Explosives such as Semtex, used by the IRA and other terrorist groups, are very much more powerful than traditional ones and are very difficult to detect, as they do not show up on normal screening devices. At the same time, it has become easier to obtain weapons.

It is thus possible for a well-organized group, convinced of the rightness of its cause, and with the belief that an act of terrorism will further it, to carry out enormous disruption, destruction and bloodshed. An air crash such as that which took place at Lockerbie in December 1988 showed this all too clearly. A bomb, which had been successfully loaded on to a plane, exploded – killing all the passengers and several residents of the town on which it crashed. It was a horrifying reminder of the power of the terrorist.

In short, we live in a world where in some parts restraints on the use of violence have broken down, and it has become easier for those who wish to use violence to do so. The mobility of terrorists, together with an increased sophistication in terrorist weapons and methods, have combined to make acts of terrorism easier to commit. The publicity that each act of terrorism gains for the terrorist makes it an ideal weapon for many powerless groups determined to bring their cause to the attention of the world.

WHY USE TERRORISM?

The first reason may be, of course, that a group actually believes that terrorism will be an effective way of achieving its aims. Its primary aim may be publicity, for instance. Terrorism is an effective way of achieving this. It may believe that the fear and tension its acts will bring will force a government to give in to its demands. In other words, the group sees terrorism as an effective *strategy* for achieving its aims. In the next chapter we will examine the use of terrorism as a strategy in more detail (see in particular pages 41-47).

It has also been argued, however, that groups and individuals turn to terrorism out of desperation. They may have a cause to which no one pays attention. The most important thing for them is to force the attention of the world on to their sufferings.

This would certainly appear to have been the case with the Palestinians who, after the establishment of Israel in 1948 and her massive victory over the surrounding Arab states in 1967, saw any chance of regaining their homeland slip even further away (see the Case Study on page 30). It was perhaps not surprising that some Palestinian groups started resorting to hijacking and other acts of terrorism in their determination to focus the eyes of the world on their cause.

Some experts on terrorism have looked at the personalities of terrorists. Is there a particular type of person who is drawn to the use of violence in this way? In practice, it has not been easy to find a typical terrorist personality, although it appears that some terrorists have joined terrorist organizations because of a deep-rooted need to have the power that terrorism provides. They may be weak or inadequate personalities, who find that only through the publicity of some dramatic act such as one of terrorism do they feel fulfilled. On the other hand, many terrorists examined by doctors have proved to be little different from the normal population.

The vast majority of terrorists have been young men aged between 18 and 30. Women play a minor role in most groups. One reporter in the Lebanon in the summer of 1986 observed how the bitter fighting between terrorist and guerrilla groups would stop each night between 9 p.m. and 2 a.m. as the men from each side gathered round television sets to watch the World Cup. The women, on the other hand, had to use these vital hours to search for their children and for food – and to bury the dead.

There have been some situations where terrorism seems to have become a form of self-defence. In the Lebanon, for example, where law and order has broken down

WHAT IS TERRORISM?

FOCUS ON....
Terrorism and nationalism

Nationalism, support for one's national group or people, has been one of the strongest forces of the past 200 years. It has been the power which has fuelled many terrorist groups. The IRA are fighting for a united Ireland. The Palestinians are seeking to regain their national homeland. There are many other cases not discussed in detail in this book. ETA is a group in Spain which hopes to create a separate state for the Basque people in the north of the country. Its campaign has now lasted almost 30 years. In Eastern Turkey, Armenian groups, notably one called ASALA (the Armenian Secret Army), have used terrorism as part of a struggle for an independent Armenia which they would unite with Soviet Armenia to the north. In

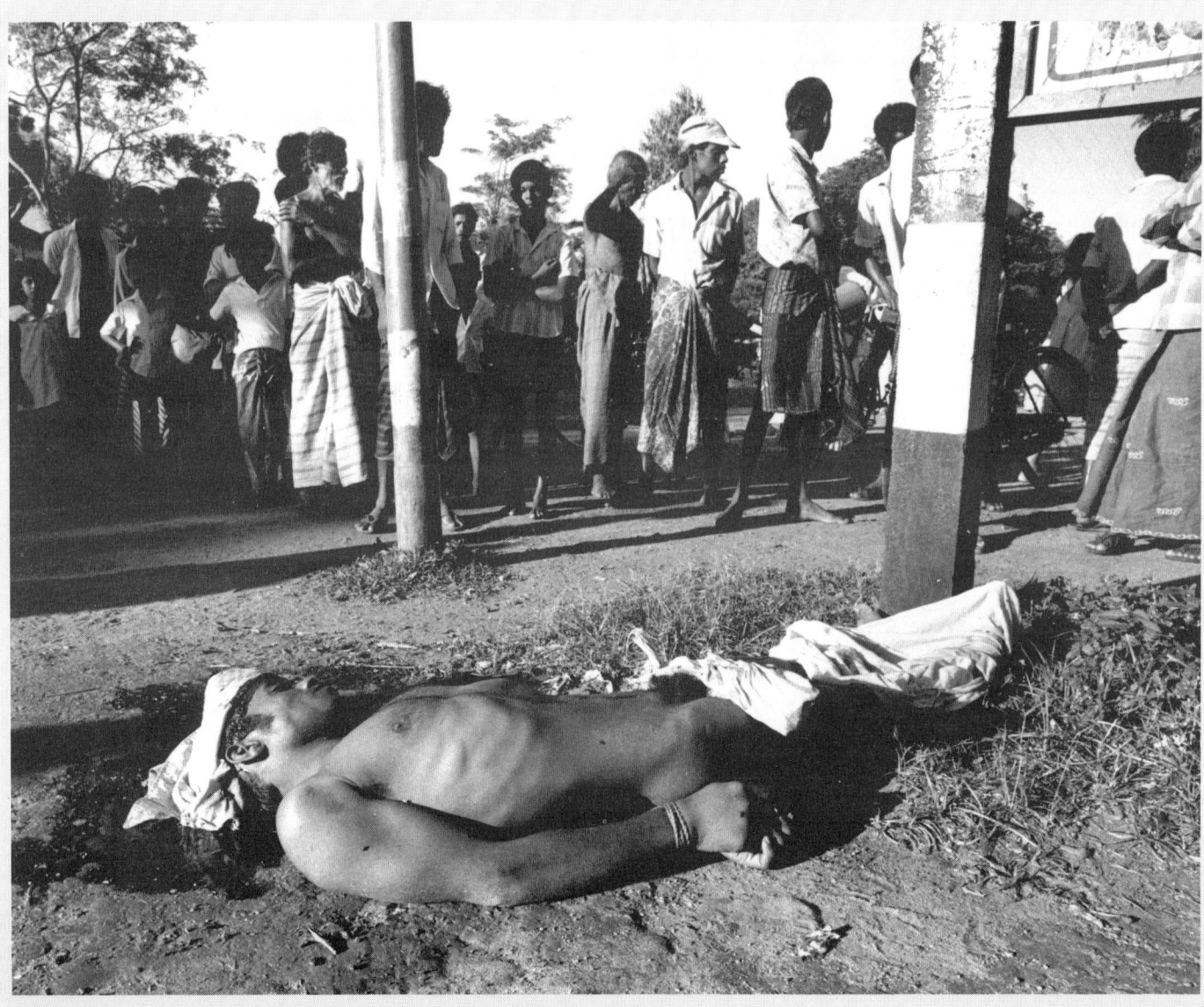

WHAT IS TERRORISM?

Sri Lanka. The bodies of victims believed to have been killed by Tamils fighting for an independent state in the north of the country.

Sri Lanka, terrorism has been used on behalf of the Tamils, a community whose roots in Sri Lanka go back a thousand years, in their struggle for a separate state in the north of the country.

These nationalist or separatist groups can make a strong emotional appeal to their followers. It is often difficult to refuse to join the struggle for fear of being seen as a traitor to the nation. The groups can put forward a clear aim, the creation of an independent national homeland. They can also point to the example of many other national groups who have achieved their independence through armed struggle. It is not surprising, therefore, that nationalist terrorist groups have been among the most successful in maintaining support and survival. Even when one group fails, another fighting for the same cause often appears to revive the struggle.

WHAT IS TERRORISM?

FOCUS ON....

Guerrillas and terrorists

The word guerrilla is used to describe armed men usually acting in small groups and working together to overthrow a government of which they disapprove. We find guerrillas acting in many parts of the world today.

Mao Zedong in China (in the 1930s and 1940s), Fidel Castro in Cuba (1950s) and Robert Mugabe in Zimbabwe (in the 1970s) were all guerrilla leaders who successfully overthrew governments and achieved power for themselves and their supporters. Guerrillas hold a variety of political beliefs. Some, such as Mao, were communists. Others have been primarily nationalists, aiming to free their country from colonial rule. Others have been strongly anti-communist, including in the 1980s the Contra guerrillas in Nicaragua, and the mujahadeen (guerrillas) in Afghanistan fighting the invading Soviet Army. What guerrillas have in common is their method of fighting, operating in small groups, often trying to build support among the local people, harassing and ambushing the government forces rather than confronting them in direct battle.

Che Guevara.

A victorious Mao Zedong proclaimed The People's Republic of China in 1949. Mao laid down strict rules about the correct behaviour of guerrillas, although these were not always followed in practice.

completely in some areas over the past ten years, a large number of groups have used terror and counter-terror in an attempt to survive in the climate of fear and disintegration. Possibly, as we have seen, the same thing has happened in some Catholic areas of Northern Ireland, where attacks on the army and police have been partly a response to the tensions of police raids and army patrols.

Once terrorism has become established as a method of fighting a particular cause it can very often become part of a tradition. In the Palestinian refugee camps, for instance, each new generation is taught that violence, often including the use of terrorism, is justified in the struggle for their lost homeland. The IRA recruits from the same families generation after generation.

TERRORISM WORLDWIDE

Terrorist acts have taken place worldwide. In the nineteen sixties Latin America appeared the centre of world terrorism, as guerrilla groups inspired by the success of Castro in seizing power in Cuba tried to overthrow governments. Many of them used terrorist tactics in the process.

Among Latin American guerrilla groups who used terrorism were the Tupermaros in Uruguay, who were involved in a number of kidnappings and assassinations, and the Montoneros in Argentina, who launched a similar campaign. Both groups invited heavy government repression and were eventually crushed.

In the late 1960s the centre of world terrorism shifted to the Middle East, where Palestinian groups used terrorism as a tactic to improve publicity and support for their cause. The Middle East continues to provide the background and support for much of the world's international terrorism. In the seventies and eighties, Western Europe also became vulnerable to terrorist attacks. The British govern-ment was involved in a bitter struggle with terrorists in both the Catholic and Protestant communities in

FOCUS ON....
Where does terrorism come in?

Many guerrillas reject the use of terrorism. Che Guevara, a Cuban guerrilla, warned that 'terrorism is generally ineffective and indiscriminate in its results, since it often makes victims of innocent people and destroys a large number of lives that would be valuable to the revolution. Mao Zedong in China insisted that correct treatment of civilians was vital if the revolution was to build support. He saw the work of the guerrillas as primarily to wear down the armed forces of the government. This fighting between guerrillas and armed forces was guerrilla warfare, not terrorism.

Guerrilla warfare, however, requires immense patience. It usually takes years to wear down the forces of a well-armed enemy. In practice, many guerrilla groups have lacked this patience. They have tried to intimidate local communities by attacking civilians or their leaders, in order to force them into supporting the guerrillas. When they are using fear in this way as one of their weapons we are right to call them terrorists.

We should be careful, however, not to use the words guerrilla and terrorist as if they were the same. We should look at the type of action carried out by the group. If it involves widespread killing of civilians, for instance, then it is probably terrorism. In short, guerrillas may be terrorists but they do not have to be.

Many of the most important guerrilla wars of the twentieth century have taken place in the countryside – in China, Africa and Latin America, for instance. However, some guerrillas have taken the struggle to the cities. They are known as urban guerrillas. In cities, terrorism is much more likely to be used in the struggle and in practice the terms urban guerrilla and terrorist have come to mean very much the same thing.

WHAT IS TERRORISM?

Northern Ireland and there were other European outbreaks, ranging from the activities of the Baader-Meinhof groups in West Germany to the Red Brigades in Italy and ETA, seeking an independent Basque state in Northern Spain. There is, in fact, virtually no part of the world which has escaped some form of terrorist act.

THE TERRORIST GROUP

Terrorist groups vary enormously in their size, stability and efficiency. At one extreme there are large guerrilla groups, numbering in the thousands and controlling their own territory, who use terrorism as one weapon in their fight against a government. In the African wars of liberation of the 1960s and 1970s there were numerous examples of civilians being killed by guerrillas either as a 'punishment' for collaborating with the government forces, or to frighten the local population into supporting the guerrilla movement. At the other extreme there are tiny terrorist groups, perhaps with only four or five members. This has been typical of West European groups such as the Baader-Meinhof gang, which carried out a number of bomb attacks in West Germany in the early 1970s, and Action Directe in France which had only a few core members. These small isolated groups are often quickly detected and rounded up by police.

Longer established and more stable terrorist groups such as the IRA may have quite a large membership – perhaps in the hundreds – but be organized in isolated cells of three to five members (for security reasons). Each cell receives orders from above and operates independently. If one cell is wiped out, as happened in the Gibraltar shootings of an IRA group in 1988, the organization, though weakened, can still continue to operate. Abu Nidal's Fateh Revolutionary Council, a Palestinian terrorist group, is believed to plant members in target countries and often wait years before using them.

In some cases, such as the Palestinians, many different groups may be using terrorism for the same cause. There are hundreds of Palestinians prepared to join small groups, which just commit one hijacking or bomb attack and then to disappear again. This is in addition to the more long-established groups such as the PFLP and Abu Nidal's Fateh Revolutionary Council, which have operated effectively over a number of years (see case study on the Palestinians for more details).

How do terrorist groups form? Many draw on existing family relationships. This has been true of both Palestinian groups and the IRA. As mentioned in the Case Study on Northern Ireland, 80 per cent of the members of the IRA have had a brother, uncle or father in the group. Abu Nidal built up his terrorist group using a network of his family relationships. Such links, by encouraging loyalty, help keep a terrorist group secure and stable.

Not all terrorist groups have such stability. Many, in fact, are full of bitter internal struggles. In 1972, a hideout of the Japanese United Red Army group was found. There were 14 bodies there – one half of the group had killed the other half. There are usually severe punishments in terrorist groups, including the death penalty for informing. Disputes between groups fighting for the same cause are also common and many end in violence. This has been true both in Northern Ireland and among the Palestinians.

On the other hand there has also been co-operation between groups from different parts of the world. An early example was the use by Palestinians of Japanese terrorists to carry out a massacre at Lod Airport in Israel in 1972. In 1988 Japanese terrorists were suspected as having been organized by Abu Nidal to carry out a bomb attack on an American club in Naples which killed five people. By this stage it appeared that there were Japanese terrorist groups ready to commit terrorism for whoever would pay them. The French group Action Directe, rounded up in 1987 after a number of assassinations, had planned their attacks with help from small groups in West Germany, Belgium and Italy. Some groups find most of their support and finance from sympathetic states.

CONCLUSION

One reason why it is so difficult to write about terrorism is that it has been used in so many different situations and in support of so many different causes. Terrorism has become, despite all the precautions taken against it, relatively easy to undertake. It is not difficult to find opportunities, weapons or causes for which to use terrorism. In the 1960s, when the current wave of terrorism began, many were sympathetic to the terrorists' aims – in particular the Palestinians, herded into refugee camps after the loss of their homeland. That sympathy was soon lost, as a bewildering variety of groups with all kinds of different grievances began to use terrorism, often doing no more than imitating groups who had gone before them. It became impossible to argue that all these causes were necessarily good ones, or that terrorism would in any way help them be achieved.

Draw up a list of situations where you feel it would be justified to use violence (in self-defence or to liberate your country from foreign rule, for example?). Do you think the use of terrorism would be justified in these cases?

Make a record, from newspapers and magazines, of recent acts of violence you consider to be terrorism. What was the cause for which the terrorists claimed to be fighting and what kinds of targets did they choose? Use your record to compare the campaigns of different terrorist groups.

Terrorism has become a major feature of today's world. Why?

What other methods might have been effective in defending or liberating? Compare methods. See p. 25 (Ireland) (Also India independence)

WHAT IS TERRORISM?

FOCUS ON....

Revolutionary groups aiming to overthrow capitalism

Many terrorist groups, particularly those in Western Europe, have been founded to overthrow the capitalist economic system. Capitalism is a system, such as exists in Western Europe, North America and Japan, in which individuals are freely able to develop their businesses with little interference from the state. Its opponents argue that such freedom leads to the development of a rich minority, who use their wealth to exercise power over the rest of the community and, through

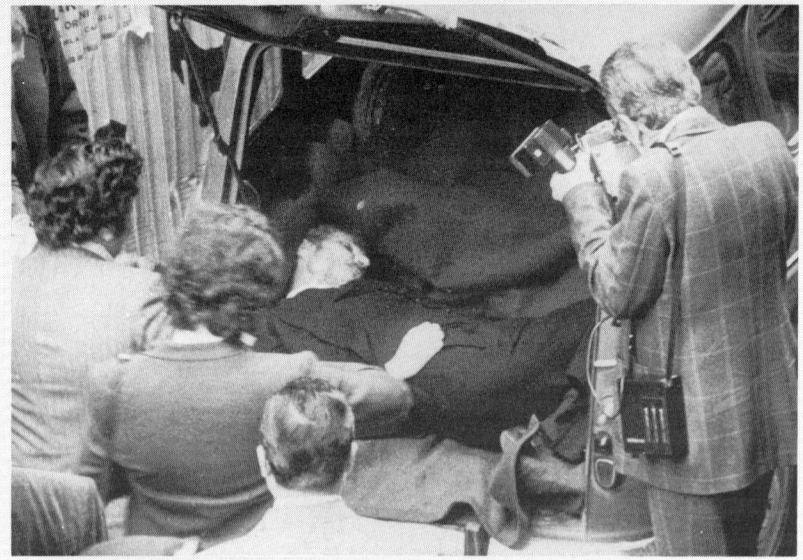

The death of Aldo Moro. The killing of Moro destroyed any sympathy the Italian public had for the Red Brigades.

A Red Brigade (Brigate Rosso) poster.

WHAT IS TERRORISM?

international business, the poor of other nations. The mass of people are left poor and without power.

A wide variety of terrorist groups have been formed to overthrow capitalism. In Western Europe they were mostly very small groups, such as the Baader-Meinhof group in West Germany and Action Directe in France both of which had very little direct contact with the masses. The most powerful of the groups were the Red Brigades in Italy. They built up a total of some seven or eight hundred members by 1978, drawn from such varied groups as students, the unemployed and criminals recruited in prison. In their struggle on behalf of the working class they committed a wide range of terrorist actions, including the murder of a former Italian Prime Minister, Aldo Moro, and numerous attacks on the police and judges. In their aim to produce a fairer and less corrupt Italian state they had, in fact, widespread support at first – but as their terror campaign continued, particularly with the murder of Moro in 1978, the nation hardened against them. By the 1980s the Italian government had gained control of the situation.

Similar groups were to be found in Latin America in the 1960s. They built on the sufferings of the poor both in the cities and in the countryside and in some countries achieved a great deal of support from all those who resented the corruption and power of the richer classes, in particular the way that the army and police defended this power. Groups such as the Tupermaros in Uruguay were popular when they began their campaigns. It was only when they turned to more brutal acts of terrorism that they lost such support and, over Latin America as a whole, the 1970s saw many guerrilla and terrorist groups crushed by determined governments.

Renato Curcio, a Red Brigades leader, at his trial. Fear of a rescue attempt was such that captured members of the Red Brigades were held in cages such as this one.

WHAT IS TERRORISM?

FOCUS ON....

Terror from the right

While the revolutionary groups described on page 16 wanted to overthrow the state, there were also groups in Europe and Latin America who claimed the right to use terrorist violence in defence of the authority of the state. We normally call this 'right wing' activity, in contrast to the 'left wing' activities of the revolutionary movements. In Europe many of these groups had their roots in German Nazism and Italian Fascism of the period 1920-1945. Fascism and Nazism glorified the nation, and stood for authority and strong leadership. Their leaders, Adolf Hitler in Nazi Germany and Benito Mussolini in Italy, were treated as superhuman. Despite the overthrow of Fascism and Nazism in the Second World War, groups drawing their support from these ideas lived on in Europe. They were racist and bitterly opposed to any movement or party fighting for workers' rights. In Germany attacks were launched on Turks who had come to find work in that country. In Italy fascist groups launched a number of bomb attacks on workers' meetings. The worst attack of all was on Bologna Railway station in August 1980, when 75 were killed and over 250 injured. One reason why these groups survived was that they often had secret supporters in the police or army who kept them from arrest.

Similar, larger, groups were found in Latin America. Here their links with the police and army were even more obvious. In El Salvador in the early 1980s large right-wing terrorist groups were tolerated by the government and, in fact, allowed to get on with the job of eliminating its opponents.

Police make spot checks on traffic in Italian cities during the height of the Red Brigade terrorist campaign.

WHAT IS TERRORISM?

Terror against Jews. Jews have been a common target of right-wing groups. Here Jews leaving a synagogue in Rome were fired on.

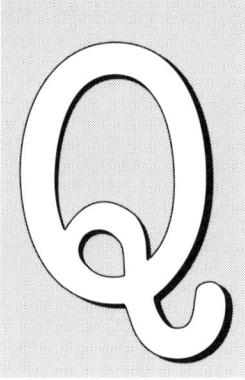

3 CASE STUDY: Terrorism in Northern Ireland

PARTITION

Catholic Ireland was ruled from the British mainland for many centuries. During this time settlers from Britain, mainly Protestant, were freely allowed to take land in Ireland and in the north-east of the island they eventually formed a majority of the population. They dominated the area both socially and economically.

By the beginning of the twentieth century the British government had accepted that some form of self-government would be given to Ireland. In the north-east, however, the Protestants were determined that they would remain loyal to Britain and, in effect, they forced the British government to divide Ireland into two. Out of the six counties of the north east, with a Protestant majority, a new province, Northern Ireland, was formed in 1921. It remained part of Great Britain. The remaining 26 counties became the independent state of Eire (or later the Republic of Ireland) ruled from Dublin. The term Loyalist is still used to describe the committed Protestant supporters of British rule, while their opponents, mostly Catholic, who wish a united Ireland are known as Republicans or Nationalists. The Loyalists are also known as Unionists (after Union with the British mainland) and prefer to use the ancient name Ulster for the province.

Over the next 40 years the Protestants in Northern Ireland consolidated their power. The Catholic minority faced widespread discrimination in housing and employment. Voting districts were often arranged so that areas with Catholic majorities were split up and attached to areas with larger Protestant populations, leaving the Catholic voters out-numbered. The British government in London, fearful of the united strength of the Protestants, did little or nothing to stop this discrimination.

THE START OF 'THE TROUBLES'

In 1968-9 the Catholics and their supporters organized a number of marches to publicize their campaign against discrimination. Many Protestants felt deeply unsettled by this and there were ambushes of some of the marches by Protestants. Later, Protestant mobs attacked Catholic working class areas. Communal tension and violence increased. The Catholics felt alone and unprotected. They realized that the overwhelmingly Protestant police force was turning a blind eye to the attacks, in some cases even joining in.

As the situation deteriorated the government of Northern Ireland called for more help. In August 1969 the British government agreed that British army units would be sent to Northern Ireland to help keep order. At first many Catholics welcomed the army. The soldiers were seen as protectors against the Protestant mobs and likely to be more sympathetic than the Protestant police forces. But as the army began trying to keep law and order, searching homes and arresting suspects, support for it dropped. To many Catholics it was a reminder of continuing British rule. They continued to feel unprotected.

CASE STUDY: TERRORISM IN NORTHERN IRELAND

THE EMERGENCE OF THE IRA

There was one group who claimed to be traditional protectors of the Catholics and yet who, in practice, had done nothing so far to defend them: the IRA (Irish Republican Army). The term IRA had first been used by Irish nationalists in the nineteenth century, but the modern IRA appeared as an actual army in the struggle for independence between 1916 and 1921. It had always opposed the partition of Ireland and from time to time after 1921 it launched campaigns against the British presence in Northern Ireland. They had always failed and by 1969 the IRA was little more than a discussion group with whom the Catholic community in Northern Ireland had little contact.

Younger members of the IRA now urged a more active role. They sensed the possibilities of building up support in the isolated Catholic communities and using force to defend them. In December 1969 a breakaway section of the IRA was formed, known as the Provisional IRA, by those prepared to take a more active role. (The remainder, the Official IRA, played a much less active role in the violence that followed and, although it did use terrorism on occasions, stopped doing so in May 1972, except in cases, it claimed, of self defence.) The long term aim of the Provisional IRA was to remove British rule from Northern Ireland.

Twenty years later the Provisional IRA still exists as a terrorist organization, despite massive and continuing police and army campaigns against it. How has it been able to do this? First it draws on very deep traditions and a history which has given it great strength. Very few Irish look back on the struggle for independence from Britain without a sense of involvement with those who fought for it. Secondly, this tradition is preserved and passed on within families. Some 80 per cent of present members of the IRA have fathers, uncles or brothers in the movement. This has given the IRA a very strong and loyal core of members. Third, it has a clear message: the removal of the British presence from Ireland. In fact, the IRA sees itself as fighting a war in order to achieve this, a war against foreign occupation. As one psychiatrist who questioned a number of IRA members who had been convicted of murder said, 'They have clear ideals and goals, they have leadership, they get strong support from other members of the group and that helps to keep them well.'

The fact that the IRA has clear ideals and a long tradition is not in itself enough to explain its continued survival. This can only be explained by looking at its role as a defender of the Catholic areas. As we saw above, the Catholic communities of Northern Ireland found themselves under intense pressures from the Protestant communities and later the British army. The Provisional IRA claimed to be defending the Catholic population from attack. Such an approach was popular. Originally there had been perhaps only 30 members of the IRA. By mid-1970 there were up to a hundred and by the end of 1970 perhaps eight hundred.

This role as defenders was made easier by the activities of the security forces, who concentrated heavily on Catholic areas in their attempt to maintain law and order. Between 1971 and 1978 there were an estimated 300,000 house searches, most in Catholic areas. Then, in 1971, the government introduced internment: that is, detention without trial. Fifteen hundred people were arrested, the vast majority of them Catholics. These policies reinforced the feeling of a community under siege. In January 1972, a march in Londonderry protesting against internment was fired on by British army paratroopers, who claimed they had been fired on first. Thirteen men were killed, seven aged under nineteen, none of whom were found to have any weapons on them. Bloody Sunday, as it came to be called, provided a major focus for hostility to the British army.

CASE STUDY: TERRORISM IN NORTHERN IRELAND

International links. The IRA has linked itself to other struggles for national freedom. In this poster, the spear and shield of the African National Congress, fighting for freedom in South Africa, is joined with symbols of the IRA. Note the machine gun at the top of the poster.

THE IRA AND ITS CAMPAIGN OF TERRORISM

Confident of some support in the Catholic working class areas the IRA expanded outwards, freely using terrorism as its main weapon against British occupation. In 1972 a campaign was launched in which the leaving of bombs in public places became the main form of terrorism. In her book *To Take Arms: A Year in the Provisional IRA*, Mary McGuire explained what the IRA was trying to do:

The intention behind the bombing campaign was to cause confusion and terror. In 1971 bomb explosions averaged three a day throughout the six counties and it was very easy to cause confusion in the centre of Belfast. There were so many targets – banks, shops, cinemas, hotels. The British had to deploy large numbers of troops there and this kept them out of the city's Catholic ghettoes. It was an obvious guerrilla tactic, allowing the volunteers

CASE STUDY: TERRORISM IN NORTHERN IRELAND

to move more freely and taking the heat off the Catholic population, who were supporting them and giving them cover. Every bomb tied up hundreds of troops and police, even if it was only a false alarm. It was possible to cause widespread disruption of the city's life with houses and offices evacuated, streets cordoned off and buses re-routed. Sometimes the Belfast Provisionals would give a succession of false alarms and then, just as the city was enjoying the lull, plant half a dozen bombs on the same day. We believed that the bombing campaign had a greater psychological effect in this way. By causing such terror we demonstrated that whatever steps the army took, the Provisionals could continue the military campaign. Half a million people in Belfast would be kept wondering where the Provisionals would strike next and would be forced to tell the British to make peace with us.

The terror we caused demonstrated that the British government could no longer govern. The campaign was aimed at economic targets, like the Electricity Board headquarters. It was intended to bring life to a halt in the Six Counties and make it so costly for the British to repair the damage that they would have to meet our demands.

In fact this campaign did not help the IRA. Catholics were as likely to be victims of the bombs as Protestants and the campaign lost the IRA much popular Catholic support. The IRA itself had expanded

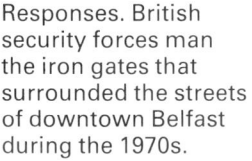

Responses. British security forces man the iron gates that surrounded the streets of downtown Belfast during the 1970s.

CASE STUDY: TERRORISM IN NORTHERN IRELAND

much too fast. Many of its 2000 members were inexperienced. Bombs went off without warning, even on occasions killing those who were trying to set them. The movement was easy to infiltrate with informers.

By 1973-4 the British Government, now ruling Northern Ireland directly, appeared to be gaining control of the situation. IRA numbers dropped, so did acts of violence. The number of terrorist related deaths fell from 467 in 1972, the worst year of all, to 216 in 1974.

The IRA, and the Catholic population, also came under pressure from Protestant terrorist groups, notably the Ulster Defence Association and the Ulster Volunteer Force. In June and July 1972 these groups were held responsible for 36 bombs, mainly aimed at the Catholic community. Between 1969 and mid-1983 Protestant (Loyalist) groups were held responsible for 613 deaths.

The IRA was forced to change its tactics. It now formed itself into small cells, often of three to five members, isolated from each other. For a period it aimed at commercial targets, hotels, shopping centres and factories, in the hope of making the economic cost of British rule too great – but this campaign again achieved little. Buildings could always be rebuilt and Catholics suffered as much as Protestants if the economy was disrupted.

In the 1980s the IRA has been more selective about its targets. It has

January 1974. A bomb explodes at the Houses of Parliament as part of the IRA campaign to spread terror to the British mainland.

CASE STUDY: TERRORISM IN NORTHERN IRELAND

concentrated on the security forces, the army and the police, the most obvious sign of the British presence in Northern Ireland. Sixty-two soldiers died in the eight years 1980 to 1987, with another 21 in 1988, eight in a single IRA attack on an army coach in August. The RUC, the Royal Ulster Constabulary, the police force of Northern Ireland, has also been a target. Twenty-three of its members were killed in 1985.

The Ulster Defence Regiment, a force raised in Northern Ireland almost entirely from the Protestant population, has also come under attack, losing almost a hundred men in the 1980s. The IRA has also attacked civil servants and judges. In August 1979, Lord Mountbatten, an uncle of the Queen, was killed by an IRA bomb which exploded in his fishing boat when he was holidaying in Ireland.

On several occasions during their campaign the IRA have extended their attacks to the British mainland. Four bombs were planted in London in March 1973, two of which went off. In the second half of 1974 there was a major wave of IRA attacks in Britain, the most horrific of which were pub bombings in Birmingham, where 21 were killed and 162 were injured in November.

In October 1984, in their most dramatic act of terrorism yet, the IRA managed to plant a bomb in the Grand Hotel, Brighton during the annual conference of Britain's ruling Conservative party. Five were killed and the Prime Minister, Margaret Thatcher, only just escaped death. There have also been attacks on British soldiers in Europe and a plan to explode a car bomb in Gibraltar during an army parade was thwarted in March 1988 when the three IRA members involved were shot dead by members of the British Special Air Service (SAS) regiment.

But in general IRA campaigns outside Northern Ireland have been shortlived. Many of the key members of the movement are well known and quickly spotted and followed when they leave Northern Ireland. The IRA has always depended on the safe support of its bases in the Catholic areas and there its roots are still deep.

1988 was not a good year for the IRA. Several of its most experienced members were shot dead by the SAS. Yet at the end of the year it still survived, with possibly some 250 members and actively involved in a continuing number of bombs and shooting incidents.

THE BRITISH RESPONSE TO THE IRA

The British government was well aware of the frustrations of the Catholic community. It realized it could only undermine support for the IRA by improving conditions for the Catholic minority and allowing Catholics to become involved in the political life of the province. In 1974 the government set up the so-called Power sharing Executive, designed to bring Catholics and Protestants together in shared government of the province. It collapsed, however, after determined opposition from Protestant Loyalists. This proved a major setback for British hopes of shared government. In the same year, the IRA was allowed to set up its own political party, Sinn Fein, in the hope that IRA supporters might be drawn into peaceful rather than violent politics. Since 1981 Sinn Fein has participated fully in elections, winning between nine and 13 per cent of the total votes. Its leader, Gerry Adams, was elected a member of the British Parliament in 1985. Adams continues, however, to defend the use of violence by the IRA.

At the same time laws such as the Fair Employment Act of 1976 attempted to make jobs equally open to both Catholics and Protestants. Money was poured into the province, £1500 million in 1985-6 alone, in the hope of improving both employment opportunities and social services. There has been some success, but the Catholic population still suffers disadvantages. In 1987, 45 per cent of Protestant school-leavers found full-time employment, as against only 32 per cent of Catholics. Worse still, the two communities still live separately, with their

CASE STUDY: TERRORISM IN NORTHERN IRELAND

The IRA provide a Guard of Honour, in this case at the funeral of Bobby Sands, who died after a hunger strike in 1981.

own housing areas and schools. The more the two communities are separated the easier it is for each to view the other as enemies.

THE SECURITY FORCES IN NORTHERN IRELAND

In the 1970s, the main responsibility for keeping law and order in Northern Ireland rested with the British army. In practice, it was almost impossible for an armed force, outsiders to Northern Ireland and clearly representing the British government, to be accepted by the Catholic community. Catholics were hardly likely to be seen to be giving the army support in the fight against terrorism and, in fact, the army became a major target for the IRA. It became clear that the army could never by itself defeat terrorism in Northern Ireland.

Gradually responsibility for law and order on the streets has been placed back with the local police force, the Royal Ulster Constabulary. This has 12,000 members. Ninety per cent are Protestant, although Catholics are better represented in the higher ranks. The force has now been modernized and appears to have wider support in the Catholic community than it once did. Far less popular among Catholics is the Ulster Defence Regiment, with 6500 members. This helps police in duties such as checking vehicles and guarding possible targets for terrorists. It is overwhelmingly Protestant. The British army, down from some 21,000 soldiers in Northern Ireland in 1972 to 10,000 in 1987, is now more involved in undercover operations and the patrolling of rural areas. Great prominence is given to one of its regiments, the Special Air

Service (SAS), which specializes in undercover work and the elimination of terrorists if caught in action.

There are special powers given to the police and army in their campaign against terrorism – powers to search houses and to detain suspects. On the whole, however, the police in Northern Ireland must arrest and convict terrorists just as they would other criminals. In other words, a suspected terrorist must be brought before a law court and evidence produced to show that he or she is guilty of an offence. (Offences include being a member of certain banned organizations, including the IRA.) As in other British criminal trials, an accused person in Northern Ireland used to have the right of trial by jury; that is 12 men and women from the local community decided on the evidence they heard whether an offence had been committed. In Northern Ireland it became difficult to uphold this. Members of juries feared what would happen to them if they convicted someone, say, from the IRA. Since 1972 the judge in terrorist trials in Northern Ireland has sat alone without a jury in the so-called Diplock Courts (named after a British judge, Lord Diplock, who first recommended them). In the Republic of Ireland such cases are also heard without juries, but with three rather than just one judge. Many in Britain have felt that this would be a fairer system.

A major problem in convicting terrorists in Northern Ireland is in finding witnesses who are prepared to give their evidence in public. Many are afraid of what will happen to them. In the early 1980s, the police relied a great deal on the so-called 'supergrasses' – informers who would give evidence in return for their own offences being overlooked. Between November 1981 and November 1983, nearly 600 people were arrested on the evidence of 'supergrasses'. However, when the trial came up, many of the 'supergrasses' retracted their evidence. In other cases, judges were unhappy about relying on such evidence if there were no other witnesses to support it.

With these difficulties in convicting terrorists it is not surprising that the security forces spend much of their efforts in house to house searches, in an attempt to find direct evidence of terrorist activity. Such searches, which in most cases prove fruitless, do nothing to help community relations. This remains the basic problem of fighting terrorism in Northern Ireland. Effective searching of areas where there may be terrorist activities inevitably involves disrupting the lives of those who have no connections with terrorism and who resent bitterly the searching of their homes.

SHOOT TO KILL?

On 11 November, 1982, a Ford Escort containing three IRA members – Gervais McKerr, Eugene Toman and Sean Burns – was driving through the town of Lurgan. According to police reports the car refused to stop when asked to by police. As another police car moved off to chase it, the police claimed they were fired on and, firing back, that they killed the three men in the car. The policemen involved had to stand trial for murder but were all acquitted. (Of 22 members of the security forces who have been tried for killings committed on duty, only two have been convicted.)

There were many doubts about the events the police had described and it was one of the incidents that a senior policeman from Britain, John Stalker of the Manchester police, was asked to investigate. When he looked into the evidence he found that the Ford Escort had never been stopped and appeared to have been fired on by a waiting policeman and the police in the car. As Stalker later wrote in his account of his investigation: 'The three officers in the police car were waiting, and they fired 108 bullets from a Sterling sub-machine gun, Ruger rifles and a handgun during a pursuit that extended over 500 yards. All the men died instantly. None was armed.'

CASE STUDY: TERRORISM IN NORTHERN IRELAND

It was incidents such as these which led many to believe that the police were adopting a shoot-to-kill policy – deliberately seeking out known members of the IRA and shooting them without any attempt being made to arrest them. This has never been publicly admitted. It would, of course, discredit the forces which allowed it to happen. There is no death penalty in Northern Ireland or the rest of Great Britain, even for the most horrific terrorist offence. Even if there was it could only be carried out after the accused terrorist had been convicted in open court.

The same issue came up in Gibraltar in March 1988. The IRA, determined on a dramatic act of terrorism to show that they were still active, planned to set off a bomb in the centre of Gibraltar with its main target the band of the resident British army regiment. The team of three IRA members was spotted and tracked and on Sunday 6 March there was some evidence that a car they had parked in Gibraltar's main square already had a bomb aboard. (In fact, the bomb was concealed in a car across the Spanish border, which would have been driven over to change place with the first parked car.) The aim of the police was to arrest the terrorists and, of course, to defuse the bomb if it were there. In order to carry out the arrest it was decided to use members of the Special Air Service regiment (the SAS) who had been flown to Gibraltar. They were in place on 6 March to follow the terrorists who, after leaving the car, moved quickly towards the border with Spain.

The events which followed are unclear. The SAS story was that the terrorists had realized they had been spotted and made movements which suggested they were either going to set off the bomb or fire at the SAS. Other versions suggest the SAS fired without warning. In any case, the three terrorists were shot dead with the SAS leaving the spot immediately.

An inquest into the deaths did support the SAS version of events, but doubts still remained about whether this version was correct and there remains some concern as to whether armed military and police units are remaining within the limits of the law, using force only in exceptional cases. The more highly trained the men carrying out the arrest are, the more they can be expected to have the experience and knowledge of how to arrest suspects without force.

Having said that the frustrations under which the police and army are acting must be understood. After all, the terrorist decides when and where he will commit violence and usually places no limit on that violence. There will be times when the police or army are justified in shooting either to protect their own lives or, as was argued in the Gibraltar case, in order to prevent a suspected bomb from being set off.

CONCLUSION

Northern Ireland provides an example of a sustained campaign of urban terrorism. The IRA could never hope to drive out the British army and other security forces by direct attack. It has been forced to resort to the use of terrorism, in the hope of undermining the will of the British government to remain. To some extent it has succeeded. The IRA has always kept a body of supporters among the Catholic community, who help it survive. The British government and people have been frustrated and wearied by the continued ability of the IRA to carry out terrorist acts. However, the British government is committed to maintaining Northern Ireland as part of the United Kingdom, unless a majority of its population want a change. At present there is no sign that they do and thus the struggle against IRA terrorism continues.

CASE STUDY: TERRORISM IN NORTHERN IRELAND

Why has the IRA proved so difficult to defeat?

Assuming that the IRA is never going to be defeated completely, what do you feel should be the long term policy of the British government towards Northern Ireland?

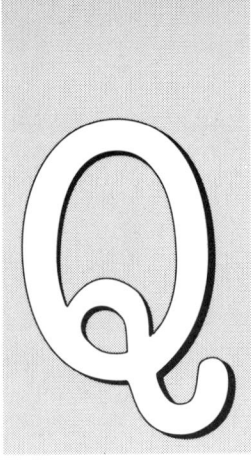

4 CASE STUDY: The Palestinians and Israel

As you have violated our land, our honour and our people, we in turn shall violate all that is yours, including your children. Our tears shall be transformed into your shed blood. The war has begun.

This message, signed 'The Palestinian Martyrs', was found on the bodies of three Palestinian terrorists shot dead by police when they launched a grenade attack at Rome airport in December 1985. Who were the Palestinian martyrs and what was their cause?

THE CREATION OF THE PALESTINIAN PROBLEM

Before 1920, Palestine, like most of the Middle East, was part of the Ottoman Empire. As the empire collapsed at the end of the First World War, Britain moved in to administer Palestine – to the dismay of the Palestinian Arabs, who had hoped for independence. Worse was to come for the Palestinians. The British government had promised that Jewish people who wished to settle in Palestine would be free to do so. (Palestine had been the original homeland of the Jews some two thousand years before, but the Jewish state had been overthrown by the Romans and its peoples scattered.)

Many thousands of Jews responded to the British offer and by 1938 there were over 400,000 Jews in Palestine. They were met with increasing hostility from the local Palestinians. The British tried to restrict further Jewish immigration but were now faced with the desperation of Jews fleeing persecution from Nazi Germany. By 1947 Britain was unable to cope any longer in Palestine. If she allowed any further Jews to come in she faced unrest from the Arab population. If she did not, she appeared to be closing her eyes to the plight of Jewish refugees attempting to start a new life in Palestine – and so soon after the horrors of the Nazi extermination camps. In despair over the results of a policy of her own making, Britain handed the problem over to the United Nations (1947).

The United Nations recommended that Palestine should be partitioned between the Jewish and Arab populations and drew up a map showing how this could be done. However, as the British started to withdraw, fighting broke out between the two communities and the Jews, well organized and armed, managed to seize large areas of the territory, proclaiming their own state of Israel in May 1948.

The surrounding Arab states sent in their armies to destroy the new state, but everywhere they were thrown back by the determined Israelis. In the chaos of the fighting some 700,000 Palestinian Arabs fled from their homes. Many of them ended up as refugees in camps in Jordan, the Lebanon, or in the Gaza Strip to the west of Israel. In another war, in 1967, Israel carried out a crushing defeat of the surrounding Arab states and this time overran the Sinai Desert and the West Bank of the Jordan. Thousands of Palestinians found themselves under direct Israeli rule – others fled to the overcrowded refugee camps. These camps, where conditions are often appalling, are a constant reminder to the world of what the Palestinians have suffered.

The Palestinians were desperate. They

CASE STUDY: THE PALESTINIANS AND ISRAEL

A Palestinian refugee camp in the Gaza Strip. It is not surprising that the conditions in these camps breed terrorism.

had seen their traditional homeland taken over by Israel. By 1967 any chance of regaining it seemed to be slipping away. For many their hostility was directed not only towards Israel but also to their fellow Arabs who seemed unable, or perhaps unwilling, to give them any effective help.

THE PLO AND ARMED STRUGGLE

In 1964 the Arab states had set up an organization to represent the Palestinians – the Palestinian Liberation Organization (PLO). Many different groups of Palestinians – including students and workers – were represented in the PLO and there was also a military section. By the late 1960s the strongest force in the PLO was a Palestinian guerrilla force known as Fateh. Its leader was Yasser Arafat, and in 1968 he was strong enough to become Chairman of the PLO, a post he was still holding over 20 years later.

It was clear that armed struggle would form a major part of the PLO's activities. Fateh continued to be the largest guerrilla group in the PLO. Thousands of Palestinians, mainly young men from the refugee camps, rushed to join it after 1967. Its main activities at this time were hit and run attacks across the Israeli borders, attacks which might be irritating to Israel but did little to harm her. To Israel, of course, these attacks were terrorism. To the Palestinians they were acts of national liberation.

However, in the desperation of 1967, other groups became established. The Popular Front for the Liberation of Palestine led by George Habash was one of these. While Fateh and Arafat had put the struggle to achieve a Palestinian state as the first aim of the PLO, the PFLP was aiming not just to remove Israel, but to achieve revolution throughout the Arab

CASE STUDY: THE PALESTINIANS AND ISRAEL

Yasser Arafat, Chairman of the PLO, a remarkable survivor of twenty years of bitterness in the Middle East.

world. It bitterly criticized those Arab leaders whom it felt had done little to help the Palestinian cause or whose military efforts had been so ineffective against the forces of Israel.

The PFLP also believed that more dramatic and effective action needed to be taken against Israel. It was they who launched the first hijackings. In July 1968 they hijacked a plane belonging to the Israeli airline, El-Al, taking it to Algeria. All the passengers were later released by the Algerians and, in fact, Israel released 16 Arab prisoners it was holding as a gesture of goodwill. After this, however, El-Al increased its security and the Israeli government introduced a policy of no negotiations over any hostages – one which still stands today.

As El-Al improved its security, gradually introducing what are probably the tightest rules of any airline in the world, the PFLP turned to other airlines, particularly those of governments seen to be supporting Israel. In September 1970 the PFLP launched five hijackings. One attempt on an Israeli jet failed. The other four, on American, Swiss and British planes, all succeeded. Three of the planes were flown to Jordan, where they were blown up once the passengers had been released.

This act was a deliberate provocation of Jordan and its ruler, King Hussein. In fact, the Palestinian groups living in Jordan were becoming a direct threat to his authority and he was not standing for it. In September 1970 he ordered his troops to move in on the Palestinians. They stood little hope against his well-trained army. Some three thousand Palestinians died and many of their refugee camps were reduced to rubble. The Palestinians had not only suffered defeat by an Arab government, they had lost an important base from which Israel could be raided by their guerrillas. The remnants of this defeat in what became known as 'Black September' fled to the Lebanon, where an attempt was made to rebuild the Palestinian forces.

It was in the years immediately following this defeat that terrorism carried out by extremist Palestinian groups was at its most intense. A shadowy group using the name Black September carried out the kidnappings at the Munich Olympics (see page 41). There continued to be hijackings of planes, the shooting of Israeli citizens and at Lod Airport in Israel in May 1972, 26 pilgrims to the Holy Land were killed when a group of Japanese terrorists, acting in collaboration with Palestinians, opened fire with machine guns. Attacks were also launched on Jordan. Its Prime Minister was assassinated by Palestinians, again acting under the name of Black September, in November 1971.

CASE STUDY: THE PALESTINIANS AND ISRAEL

One of the first PFLP hijacks, of a Swissair plane in 1970. The passengers have been released but the plane was blown up shortly afterwards.

THE MOVE TO LEBANON

The main headquarters of the PLO was now the Lebanon. The Fateh guerrillas moved into the southern part of the country, the part closest to the Israeli border and there set up what was almost a separate state. Palestinians and other sympathizers could be trained, and raids and rocket attacks could be made across the Israeli border.

While supporting these raids, the leadership of the PLO condemned many of the terrorist actions of the more extreme Palestinian groups. Yasser Arafat realized that the best hope of regaining a Palestinian state was to maintain good relations with the other Arab states. In the 1973 Yom Kippur war with Israel, the surrounding Arab states had for the first time held their own against Israeli troops, and so there was now some hope that they might be able to give effective help to the Palestinians. In 1977 Arafat agreed to meet the man who had inflicted so much suffering on the Palestinians in Black September, King Hussein of Jordan. Good relationships with the Arab states also brought in money. Fateh received between 150 and 200 million dollars in 1975 alone from sympathetic Arab states. It continued to be the dominant force in the PLO.

However, the PLO's base in the Lebanon was not secure. The country itself was made up of two major communities, one Christian and one

CASE STUDY: THE PALESTINIANS AND ISRAEL

Muslim Nasserite urban guerrillas patrol the streets of Beirut.

Islamic (Muslim). But even these were split. The Muslims, for instance, were divided into Sunnis and Shias, representing a centuries old divide in their faith reflected across the Muslim world. There was also a third Muslim group, the Druzes, found only in the Lebanon. There were already tensions between the communities as the Christians occupied a dominant political and economic position in the state which was resented by the Muslims.

The Palestinians brought all kinds of new tensions. They were a large and armed group in what was already an unstable country. To make things worse, Lebanon now found itself under attack from Israel, as Israeli troops and planes hit back after Fateh raids. In 1975 the country cracked under the strain and civil war broke out between Christians and Muslims. The Palestinians, many of whom, of course, were already armed, became drawn into the fighting on the Muslim side. As law and order broke down, the neighbouring state of Syria decided to intervene in order to bring back stability. Syria invaded in support of the Christians and successfully occupied the north of the country, in effect bringing defeat to the Palestinians.

More serious defeat for the Palestinians then came from the Israelis. Israel, tired of the Palestinian raids, invaded the Lebanon first in 1978 and then even more ruthlessly in 1982. Its troops pushed the Palestinians northwards up into the capital city, Beirut. 11,000 Palestinian guerrillas were eventually trapped in the city and were steadily bombarded by the

CASE STUDY: THE PALESTINIANS AND ISRAEL

Massacre in the refugee camps. The aftermath of killings of Palestinians by Christian militiamen in the Lebanon, 1982.

Israeli army. There was no hope for them. They were forced to evacuate by sea. They left, defiant, many still carrying their arms. Arafat himself went on the 30 August. It was another massive setback for the Palestinians.

There was a horrific sequel to the evacuation. On 16 September, Israeli troops stood by as extremist Christian groups moved into two Palestinian refugee camps which remained, Shatila and Sabra, and massacred several hundred of their inhabitants.

For the moment it looked as if the Palestinian cause was now doomed. The PLO had no remaining base near to Israel. There seemed no effective way of publicizing its cause. Although some Palestinian groups continued to use terrorism (see page 37), it appeared to achieve nothing. The Arab states said that they continued to support the Palestinian cause but were not prepared to risk conflict with Israel to further it.

THE *INTIFADA* AND ARAFAT'S RENUNCIATION OF TERRORISM

Then suddenly the situation was changed. Many thousands of Palestinians still remained under Israeli control. In the Gaza Strip, for instance, a small stretch of territory between Egypt and Israel taken over by Israel in 1967, there are 550,000 Palestinians, two-thirds of them refugees. In the West Bank, also taken over by Israel in the 1967 war, there are another 850,000. In December 1987, riots broke out against Israeli control. The Israelis, attempting to repress the unrest, sent in their army.

CASE STUDY: THE PALESTINIANS AND ISRAEL

This just made matters worse and soon there was a major uprising under way – the *intifada*. A year later, although the Israelis had achieved back some control, the spirit of revolt was not dead.

The *intifada* brought the Palestinian cause back into the headlines. The refugee camps with all their squalor were back on the television screens. So too were the activities of the Israeli army, which were often brutal. Here at last was an opportunity for the Palestinians to exploit the worldwide sympathy the uprising had brought them.

Yasser Arafat, still the leader of the PLO after the setbacks and humiliations of the previous years, then made an important move. In November 1988 he declared an independent state of Palestine, accepting, however, that this would have to exist alongside Israel. (Before this most Palestinians had refused to accept that Israel had any right to exist.) In December he went further. He knew he would have the support of the Arab states for his new policy. What was really vital for him was the support of the West. Many Western nations, in particular the United States, had supported Israel and had refused to talk to the PLO on the grounds that it was a terrorist organization. Now Arafat publicly renounced the use of terrorism. The Western nations accepted his word. Soon the United States and Britain were talking to him. The change of policy by the United States was particularly important because she had been the firmest supporter of Israel throughout the years and a steadfast opponent of the PLO.

Immense problems in setting up a Palestinian state still remain. Israel is likely to oppose it to the last and it remains difficult to see how suitable territory for this state will be regained from Israeli control. And anyway, the relationship between the PLO and the United States had broken down again by mid-1990.

Yasser Arafat's survival as head of the PLO over 20 years has been extraordinary. His life has been threatened so often that he never sleeps in the same bed two nights running. Many of his enemies are Palestinians who feel that he has not been ruthless enough in the fight for a Palestinian homeland, one which these Palestinians would hope would involve the total destruction of the state of Israel.

Arafat refused to allow these Palestinian extremists too much influence in the PLO and often condemned their acts of international terrorism. As a result they have had to look elsewhere for support and they have found it in several governments in the Middle East, including Syria, Iraq and above all, Colonel Gadhaffi in Libya.

COLONEL GADHAFFI AND THE SUPPORT OF TERRORISM

The case of Colonel Gadhaffi is unlike any other in the world of terrorism. His country, Libya, is small – with some three million inhabitants – but thanks to oil revenue it is relatively rich. Gadhaffi has used the money to support, finance, arm and encourage a wide variety of terrorist activities across the world. Gadhaffi would claim that his main targets were Israel, those Western nations such as the United States which support her, and the moderate Palestinian groups who should have tried harder to destroy Israel. He has also supported the IRA, providing most of its arms and smaller terrorist groups such as Action Directe in France, and others in Italy and West Germany.

Unlike other governments and leaders who have supported terrorist groups, Gadhaffi has acted fairly openly and seems to take satisfaction in what he is doing. He likes to see himself as a fervent supporter of all those claiming to seek 'liberation'.

Gadhaffi's support for the Palestinians' cause has focussed on the more extreme Palestinian groups, those who have fallen out with Yasser Arafat and the leadership of the PLO. He has even gone so far as to plan the assassination of Arafat himself. A group of Fateh rebels who turned against Arafat in

CASE STUDY: THE PALESTINIANS AND ISRAEL

1983 was reported to have received 30 million dollars from Gadhaffi.

The most notorious of the Palestinian groups helped by Gadhaffi has been that run by Abu Nidal. Abu Nidal was born in Palestine in the late 1930s. He was originally a member of the PLO and later, it is believed, connected with Black September. He then moved to Iraq where he was supported by the Iraqi government in building up a group, now known as the Fateh Revolutionary Council, made up of them young Palestinians – many of them related to him. His group is bitterly opposed to the PLO, whom it considers far too moderate. Attacks have been launched on PLO offices in Syria, Italy, Pakistan, France and Britain, as well as on that old enemy of the Palestinians, Jordan.

Eventually, the Iraqi government, reluctant to be seen to be sponsoring terrorism, broke with Abu Nidal. But Abu Nidal quickly found support from both Syria and Libya. By 1988 it appeared that the activities of the group were being largely financed by Gadhaffi. These activities had expanded by this time to include attacks across Europe, particularly against American targets, making the group one of the most ruthless operating out of the Middle East. Many believed that the group was behind the Lockerbie air disaster bomb.

Gadhaffi has supported such a wide variety of terrorist groups that he has become distrusted by everyone. To most Arab states he is an embarrassment. The only result of his activities has been to increase instability in the Middle East. In April 1986, after a number of terrorist incidents against American targets, the American government retaliated by bombing Libya. For two years Gadhaffi appeared more restrained in his support of terrorism but by 1988 his activities appeared to have resumed.

Colonel Gadhaffi, speaking on television after the US bombing of Libya.

CASE STUDY: THE PALESTINIANS AND ISRAEL

IRAN AND SHI'ITE TERRORISM

In 1979 there was major upheaval in Iran. Its pro-West leader, the Shah, was forced into exile and the country came under the rule of its religious leaders, headed by Ayatollah Khomeini. They came from the Shia branch of Islam, as did the majority of the Iranian population, and once in power they insisted on returning to what they saw as the traditional values of Islam. These included the restriction of religious freedom, the return to the traditional Islamic punishments such as amputations, and the exclusion of women from public life. Khomeini enforced his rule harshly.

The triumph of the Shias in Iran gave hope to Shias in other Arab countries, in particular in the Lebanon. The Shias there have been a large and growing part of the Muslim community, but they are mostly poor. Originally most lived in the countryside, but in recent years they have drifted to the towns – making up a discontented minority. As law and order broke down in the Lebanon in the 1970s, the Shias formed their own guerrilla group, Al Amal. Its main strength lay in West Beirut and the South of the Lebanon and, not surprisingly, it looked to Iran for support (as well as to Syria, whose government was controlled by Shias).

In 1982 a number of groups broke away from Al Amal. Two in particular became quickly known, Al Jihad al Islami (Islamic Holy War) and Hizbollah (the Party of God). These received strong support from Iran. They fought not only other groups within the Lebanon (including in 1989 Al Amal itself) but were bitterly opposed to the West. They saw the West not only as the main supporter of Israel but believed that the Western way of life was a direct

The crew of TWA's flight 847 during the Beirut hijacking of 1985. The three men were held hostage in the plane's cabin for 16 days.

CASE STUDY: THE PALESTINIANS AND ISRAEL

The destruction after the massive explosion in the US Marines' headquarters, October 1983.

threat to traditional Islam.

The first act of terrorism of Al Jihad al Islami was to attack the American and French Embassies in Beirut (March 1983). In October 1983 they launched attacks on the headquarters of French and American troops stationed in Beirut as a peace-keeping force. A massive six ton bomb killed 241 American marines and in the French attack 58 French soldiers died. Bomb attacks were carried out in Kuwait in December 1983, probably in protest against that country's support of Iran's enemy, Iraq. Al Jihad al Islami also hijacked a TWA (American) airliner in June 1985 and held it at Beirut airport for several weeks, killing one American during the ordeal.

In Britain, Hizbollah is perhaps best known for its kidnapping of Western hostages, the most famous of whom, Terry Waite, was kidnapped in January 1987 – while on a mission to free hostages already taken. Iranian support for these groups was so obvious that the main efforts to release them had to be made via the Iranian government. The United States government was even prepared to secretly provide Iran with arms in order to get its hostages in the Lebanon released.

Iran has used its own terrorist groups as well. One of these, the Guardians of the Islamic Revolution, has been used to attack Iran's enemies directly. It claimed responsibility for the placing of the bomb which blew up the Pan-Am Boeing over Lockerbie in December 1988, claiming that it was in revenge for the shooting down of an Iranian airliner in the Persian Gulf by the United States navy.

In 1989 Ayatollah Khomeini, shortly before his death, declared that the book *The Satanic Verses*, by the British author Salman Rushdie, was so deeply insulting to the Islamic religion that Rushdie should be killed. Iranians and their supporters were urged to carry out this act of terrorism. As a result Rushdie was forced into hiding.

CASE STUDY: THE PALESTINIANS AND ISRAEL

Do you believe the Palestinians were justified in using terror? What have they achieved by their use of terrorism over the past 20 years?

What is the best way to deal with states, such as Libya, which support the use of international terrorism?

5 Terrorism: Strategies and Effects

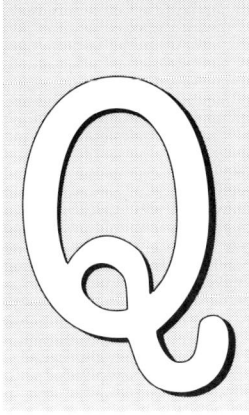

TERRORISM AND PUBLICITY

Munich, West Germany, September 1972. The nations of the world were gathered for the Olympic Games. In the middle of the Games, terrorists from the Palestinian group, Black September, launched an attack. Their target was the team of athletes from Israel. Two were killed, another 11 kidnapped. The West German police moved in. There was a shoot out. All the athletes were killed, as were five of the eight terrorists.

Some time later a spokesman for the Palestinians summed up the reason for the attack.

> We recognize that sport is the modern religion of the Western world. We knew that the people of England and America would switch their television sets from any programme about the plight of the Palestinians if there was a sporting event on another channel. So we decided to use their Olympics, the most sacred ceremony of this religion, to make the world pay attention to us. We offered up our human sacrifices to your gods and television. And they answered our prayers. From Munich onwards nobody could ignore the Palestinians or their cause.

Terrorists seek publicity. They can achieve nothing without it. First, it brings the attention of the world to their cause. The Palestinians have perhaps been the most successful group in achieving this. After Palestinian groups hijacked a number of planes in the late 1960s, the world as a whole became aware for the first time of the circumstances in which the Palestinians had lost their homeland. Despite the brutality of their actions, many people developed sympathy for the Palestinian cause and came to realize the desperation that lay behind many of the acts of terrorism.

Secondly, publicity not only brings awareness of a cause but also of the group fighting for it. Terrorism is an easy way for a small and weak group to appear strong. The IRA, for instance, on occasions when it has suffered a severe setback, such as when eight of its members were killed in a shoot out in 1987, will often plan a dramatic act of terrorism to show that it can still operate effectively. In Paris, in August 1981, the International Hotel was bombed. No less than six groups claimed to have done it, so desperate was each group to show that it was a force to be reckoned with.

One way for a group to show that it is effective is to choose an event which is of special importance for the community it is attacking. The Olympic Games is one good example. Ever since they were first founded in ancient Greece, the success of the Olympic Games depended on nations putting aside their conflicts and competing with each other peacefully. To bring an act of violence into the middle of the Games was, for the Palestinians, a sign of their power to challenge even the most 'sacred' of events. The IRA bomb attack at Enniskillen on a Remembrance Sunday had a similar impact.

As we saw in Chapter Two, an essential aim of most terrorist groups is to spread fear. There is an old Chinese proverb, 'Kill one, frighten a thousand'. It is vital that the terrorist gets publicity for each act of killing so that the community as a whole is frightened.

TERRORISM: STRATEGIES AND EFFECTS

Attack at Munich, 1972. An armed Palestinian gunman guards the captured hostages.

TERRORISM: STRATEGIES AND EFFECTS

> **TALKING POINT**
>
> ## The terrorist and the media
>
> It was the 5 May 1980. For five days the Iranian Embassy in London had been under seige after six gunmen had seized 26 hostages and held them there. Suddenly there was an explosion. The building was being stormed, successfully as it turned out, by the SAS.
>
> At the same time as the explosion there was a scream. Most people assumed it came from an injured hostage or one of their relatives waiting anxiously outside the Embassy. It was later claimed that it was in fact the BBC reporter Kate Adie yelling for everyone to get out of the way so that she could get on with her reporting.
>
> The drama of terrorism makes excellent news and, as we have seen, this is exactly what the terrorists want. The terrorists use the media for their own ends and the many journalists and television reporters, competing against each other, cannot afford not to report each story as dramatically as possible.
>
> During the hijack of an American plane in Beirut in June 1985, the three major United States news networks devoted two-thirds or more of their early evening news to the story. On four nights one of the networks, ABC, spent less than two minutes on the rest of the nation's and world's news. American newsmen were even allowed by the hijackers to come in to interview the hostages while they were still in captivity.
>
> Many questions are posed by this. Are there any controls which should be placed on the reporting of terrorist incidents? In 1988 the British government did impose restrictions on the reporting of terrorism. The BBC and other television companies were banned from broadcasting interviews by those representing the IRA and some other terrorist organizations. Would this actually help stop terrorism?
>
> Some argued that not only was it an unjustifiable restriction on freedom of speech, but that the best way to increase public revulsion against terrorism was to hear terrorists publicly trying to justify their actions.
>
> There are certainly cases where control of the media is justified. This is particularly the case during negotiations for the release of hostages. Often the terrorists who are holding the hostages have radios and can listen in to broadcasts. If, to take an example, the activities of the police or armed forces are freely reported, the terrorists may gain useful information, allowing them to defend themselves against attack. However, with the sophistication of modern news gathering techniques it is, in practice, almost impossible for a government to close off a terrorist group from publicity. Even the Chinese government lacked the power to stop international reporting of its own massacre of students in Beijing in June 1989. The alliance between the terrorist and the news media looks set to continue.

TERRORISM AND FEAR

It is frightening to live in a community where you know a terrorist attack may happen at any minute. Dervla Murphy, an Irish writer, who cycled around Northern Ireland in 1976, captured the atmosphere in Belfast well.

> The prim looking young woman ahead of you carrying a plastic bag just might be on her way to blow up Marks and Spencers. Or the neatly dressed respectable elderly man carrying a tidy brown paper parcel just might be going to hide it in that pub towards which you are heading. Can people really get used to living with this sort of thing?
>
> After ten days I fancied that I had become reasonably immune to it. Then one evening as I was writing in a friend's empty house a door banged upstairs and for the next five minutes I could scarcely breathe, so violently was

my heart hammering. Yet in other parts of the world I simply do not react to sudden loud noises.

On an international level the impact of fear can be even more dramatic. In 1985 and 1986, United States civilians and servicemen were the victims of a series of terrorist attacks in Europe. (One result was that the United States bombed Libya, which was believed to be behind many of the attacks.) Trips to Western Europe by United States citizens fell by 25 per cent and to Greece and Egypt by 50 per cent. It was estimated that 1.8 million United States citizens cancelled overseas trips or changed their journeys. Such is the power of fear.

HOW DOES A TERRORIST GROUP HOPE TO USE FEAR TO ACHIEVE ITS ENDS?

In Chapter Two we defined terrorism as the use of fear as a weapon to achieve political change. How does the terrorist believe that fear will be an effective weapon?

In some cases terrorists hope to use fear as a means of forcing a government to give in to its immediate demands. An example of a successful use of fear in this way came in Austria in September 1973, when a group of Palestinian terrorists seized some Jews who had emigrated from the Soviet Union and were on their way to Israel. They threatened to kill them unless the Austrian government closed a camp where Jews who had just arrived from the Soviet Union had been allowed to stay. The Austrian government gave in. There have been many less public deals by which governments have given in to the demands of terrorists. The West German government was rumoured, for instance, to have paid five million dollars to have German hostages held in the Lebanon released.

Many governments, however, refuse to make any such deals. This is the firmly held position of the British government, for instance. They argue that by giving in to one terrorist attack, they would simply encourage more. The Kuwaiti government stood firm in a similar way in the hijack case we described in Chapter One. On the whole, increasing experience of terrorism shows that governments who do negotiate with terrorists quickly become seen as 'soft' targets all the more vulnerable to terrorism in the future.

Many terrorist groups argue that the spread of fear in a community will lead to its breakdown. This seems to have been the aim of the IRA in its campaign of 1972, (see page 22) for instance. It is not clear what exactly the terrorists expect to happen. Perhaps the community under attack will beg its government to surrender. Perhaps law and order will break down to such an extent that the terrorists will be able to take control.

In practice, this does not often happen. The IRA campaign of 1972 simply caused mass revulsion, in particular among the Catholic population whom the IRA relied on for support. In Italy in 1978, the terrorist campaign by the Red Brigades culminated in the kidnapping and death of Aldo Moro, a successful and popular politician. His death did not cause breakdown but brought the Italian people together against the Red Brigades in a way no other issue had done. There are many cases where a terrorist campaign has simply led to the strengthening of government, rather than its collapse. In Latin America in the 1960s many terrorist groups were crushed by the determined power of governments they had hoped to weaken and overthrow. Many terrorist groups have proved helpless in the face of the destructive power of the modern state.

On the other hand there are cases where terrorists have used fear successfully. For example, peacekeeping forces sent from the United States and several European nations to the Lebanon were the targets of massive bomb attacks by Shia terrorist groups on them in 1983. The United States lost 241 marines in one attack in October 1983 alone. The peacekeeping forces were quietly withdrawn the following year. It is in this kind of case, where a government or

TERRORISM: STRATEGIES AND EFFECTS

Ruins in Libya, the aftermath of US bombing raids there, 1985. Is it justified to deal with terrorism by counterattacks of this type?

its forces are isolated in a foreign country, that terrorism committed on behalf of the local inhabitants against them seems to have most effect. Few nations are prepared to take the continued strain of fighting terrorism in a foreign country where they have little or no local support.

THE COST OF TERRORISM

The first price we pay for terrorism is in lost human lives. In recent years the death toll of terrorism has risen with the increasing use of bombs planted on aircraft. 738 people died from such bombs between June 1985 and December 1988, 329 in an attack on an Air India Boeing in June 1985 and nearly 300 in the Lockerbie air disaster of December 1988. To look at another case, 1982 people died in Northern Ireland as a result of terrorism between 1970 and 1979 and 70 or 80 a year have died since then. In countries such as the Lebanon, where there has been extensive terrorism and counter-terrorism, the numbers of victims must be in the thousands.

The terrorist is not just concerned with killing individuals but with spreading the impact of each killing to the community as a whole; this impact can be immense. In her book *Fortune's Hostages* Caroline Moorehead gives a vivid picture of how life changed in Uruguay, a small country in Latin America, as the result of a terrorist campaign launched by the Tupermaros.

> Ordinary daily life in Uruguay changed. Because the Tupermaros were the sons and daughters of the middle class, middle class Uruguayans became wary and suspicious of their friends and particularly their friends' children. The white sandy beaches that run for 250 miles along the coast were empty of tourists. Punta el L'Este and Pirapolis, the smart resorts that had drawn so many Latin American visitors, were abandoned.
>
> The richer Uruguayans padlocked their large villas in Carasco, left the gardens to turn into a jungle of tropical

TERRORISM: STRATEGIES AND EFFECTS

Disaster at Lockerbie, December 1988. The front of the Pan Am airliner destroyed by a terrorist bomb as it flew over Scotland. All passengers and crew died.

plants and moved to the anonymity of city apartments – where they put false names on the doorbells and sweltered through the summer heat, too fearful even to visit the cafes at night. By 6.30 in the evening there was no one about. Restaurants and nightclubs closed down.

One major result of a terrorism campaign is thus the breakdown of trust within a community. No one knows who the terrorists may be or who sympathizes with them. As a result there is a breakdown in normal human relationships.

At the same time, governments will strengthen their powers in order to deal with terrorism. They will often restrict human rights, giving themselves more power to search houses, arrest suspects and hold them without trial, close down newspapers which offer favourable publicity to terrorists and so on. We will discuss these restrictions in Chapter Six.

Lastly, there is an enormous economic cost of terrorism. As we have seen hijacking became a major form of terrorism in the late 1960s. Airports throughout the world had to introduce screening devices to pick out hijackers or their weapons. In the United States, during the period 1973-6, an estimated $194 million was spent on screening. Machines which might detect Semtex could cost a million dollars each. In 1988 the British government was spending one and a half million pounds a day in Northern Ireland on maintaining the police and armed forces and at that time had had to pay out more than £650 million in compensation for those who had suffered personal injury or damaged property in the unrest. The government of the Irish Republic estimated that the violence had lost it one and a half billion pounds in lost tourism between 1969 and 1983, and that an extra one and three-quarter billion pounds had been spent on maintaining security.

TERRORISM: STRATEGIES AND EFFECTS

CONCLUSION

It is clear from what we have just said that a terrorist campaign does have an enormous impact on a community. The behaviour of everyone in the community is changed either by the restrictions imposed by the government, by their own fears, or by the breakdown of trust in the community. However, such changes seldom benefit the terrorist group or the cause for which it is fighting. This has perhaps been the major lesson we have learned from the use of terrorism over the past 20 years. Yasser Arafat, Chairman of the Palestinian Liberation Organization, recognized this when he renounced the use of terrorism as a weapon by the Palestinians. Twenty years of terrorism had done nothing to bring a Palestinian state into existence and had prevented the PLO from gaining the support of powerful nations of the West such as the United States and Britain.

'Nobody gains, we all lose from a campaign of terrorism.' Do you agree?

Has terrorism proved an effective way of achieving what its users have hoped to achieve?

'Terrorism would never be used if there was no publicity about it.' Do you agree? If so, is it justifiable to place restrictions on the reporting of terrorist incidents?

6 The fight against terrorism

THE STATE VERSUS THE TERRORIST

When a state is faced by acts of terrorism from within, there are several ways it can react. It may believe that the terrorists' cause is justified and thus be prepared to give in to their demands. In practice most states are reluctant to do this as they know it will weaken their authority and suggest that they are vulnerable to terrorist pressure. On the other hand, many governments under extreme pressure have made deals with terrorists.

The opposite extreme is to launch a major campaign of counterattack. One of the most brutal of such campaigns was that launched by the Iranian government in 1981 against a variety of terrorist groups which opposed the new government of Ayatollah Khomeini. At least 2500 suspects were executed; there were widespread allegations of torture, and a massive clampdown on political activity. In terms of crushing the terrorists, the campaign was successful – but the result was a dictatorship. In Latin America government campaigns of this brutal nature have destroyed terrorist groups. In the process, of course, thousands of innocent people suffer and a military dictatorship may be established, as happened in Argentina under General Galtieri (1976-83).

For a democratic state, neither of these options are possible. A democratic state believes that change can take place peacefully. The people are free to elect a government to pass laws on their behalf. These laws will be enforced by a police force which, ultimately, is under public control. Anyone accused of breaking the law is entitled to a fair and public trial, with the right to be tried by an independent judge or jury. A truly democratic government also guarantees human rights for all its members. Such rights would include freedom of speech, freedom of movement, and freedom from arrest without cause.

Terrorists are not elected. They appoint themselves. They use violence or the threat of violence to achieve their aims, rather than the elected parliament or other body which makes laws. In carrying out violence they are destroying the human rights of their victims – rights to live in peace, liberty and free of cruel treatment.

If a democratic government gives in to the threat of terrorism from within it can be argued that it is betraying the ideals of democracy. Similarly, a government is betraying democratic ideals if it responds by a campaign of mass repression. Such a campaign will depend on mass arrests of suspects, the widespread searching of private homes, and possibly the use of torture to extract information. All these are denials of the human rights on which a democratic society is based.

A democratic society under threat from terrorism is thus presented with an extraordinarily difficult challenge. How can it defeat terrorism, a threat to the ideals on which democracy is based, without betraying these same ideals?

There are certain policies which seem to be essential. First, it must be clear that everyone in the society has full access to democratic rights, including equal opportunity to share in political life, schooling, employment and access to housing. So long as one part of the community, members of one race or religion, for

THE FIGHT AGAINST TERRORISM

Security forces carry out a surveillance operation at Heathrow Airport, not the sort of welcome travellers normally expect.

Security checks have become an everyday part of life. This is a check at Frankfurt Airport. It was, in fact, through this airport, that the bomb which caused the Lockerbie disaster was smuggled onto the plane.

Q THE FIGHT AGAINST TERRORISM

FOCUS ON....

Hostages

Because Flight 840 was late we had to wait an extra half hour in the lounge . . . This extra wait was an anxious time and two things upset me before we got on the plane. I noticed an American lady with four young children who seemed very happy and excited about their trip. I then realized with a shock that something dreadful could happen to them if anything went wrong. I love children and I wanted to tell the lady not to travel on this flight. But when I thought of our Palestinian children who had nothing in life, I felt a bit stronger and braver.

The second incident was in the bus going out to the plane. A man sat next to me and asked me where I was from and I let him know I was from Bolivia. Then he told me he was a Greek returning to Athens after spending 15 years in Chicago and that his widowed mother would be waiting for him at the airport.

That was another shock. I felt it particularly because we Palestinians know what it is to be away from one's country and I too had a widowed mother waiting for me at home.

This passage comes from *My People Shall Live* by Leila Khaled, a Palestinian who unsuccessfully tried to hijack an El-Al (Israeli) airliner in 1970. Her plan, with another hijacker who was shot dead in the attempt, was to take over the airliner and hold the passengers hostage – including those she had spoken to.

Taking hostages has become one of the most common forms of terrorism. Hostages have either been taken in large groups, as on an aircraft, or as individuals – as has happened in the Lebanon where single Europeans have been held by terrorist groups. The demands of the hostage takers vary. Sometimes it is for money. This was a common event in Latin America in the 1960s and 1970s, where businessmen were held hostage until their companies had paid up. Perhaps the most usual demand of the hostage takers is for the release of prisoners, as we saw in the case of the Kuwaiti hijacking.

Hostages are placed in a horrifying position. In aircraft, provided with food and other facilities for only a short flight, conditions of fear and discomfort become intense. Often the aircraft is held for days at an airport in a hot climate. It is not surprising that many hostages are haunted by their experiences for months or even years after they have been released.

The governments who have to negotiate with hijackers are also put under severe pressures. In some cases the situation reaches a state of extraordinarily high emotion. Perhaps the extreme example of this was the hijacking to Beirut of a TWA (American) airliner in June 1985. The American news media built up the incident as if it was a national crisis, driving out all the rest of the world's news.

There was little the American government could do to solve the crisis. The hostages were taken from the plane and hidden in West Beirut, making a rescue attempt impossible. The hostages (except for one who was killed) were eventually set free when the Israeli government – under American pressure – released Palestinian prisoners. This 'giving in' was forgotten in the emotional atmosphere when the victims of the hijacking were welcomed back to the United States as heroes.

Occasionally it is possible to release hostages by force, using specially

The return of hostages. These are the released hostages from the TWA Boeing held in Beirut in 1985. American Vice-President George Bush welcomes them to freedom.

THE FIGHT AGAINST TERRORISM

trained groups. The most famous example (later made into a film) was the Israeli rescue of hostages held at Entebbe Airport after an Air France plane bound for Israel had been hijacked there in June 1976. Hostages held in the takeover of the Iranian Embassy in London by a group seeking independence for the Iranian province of Khuzistan in April 1980 were also released when the Embassy was stormed by the SAS. However, there have also been dreadful failures, the worst of which was an attack by an Egyptian commando force on a plane hijacked to Malta by the Abu Nidal group. The Egyptians acted without Maltese support and 59 hostages were killed.

The opposite extreme is to give in to the hijackers in order to have hostages released, and this has been done by many governments. On page 44 we described how the Austrian government gave in to demands to close a Jewish transit camp in order to save hostages. Large sums of money have been paid by European governments to have hostages held in the Lebanon released.

For governments who neither wish to risk using force or to give in to the hijackers' demands the only solution lies in sitting out the hijack. Many governments have now gained a lot of experience of doing this. The most important thing is to settle the situation down and then to open communications with the hijackers. It has been found that the longer the siege lasts the more likely the hijackers and hostages are to build up good relationships with each other and thus the less likely the hijackers are to use force against the hostages. The aim, of course, is to persuade the hijackers to give in without harming the hostages. This can be done by just wearing them down by maintaining steady pressure on them. In the Kuwaiti hijack the terrorists seemed to have been specially trained against such techniques and held out until they escaped in Algeria.

Whatever governments do in practice, the public line most hold is that they will not negotiate to release hostages. The British government has taken a particularly firm line on this in recent years. It is a difficult line to hold in view of the understandable pressures from friends and families of those held as hostages but it does seem the only road to take in order to discourage further incidents.

Rescuing hostages. SAS troops storm the Iranian Embassy in London, successfully releasing 19 hostages who had been held there for six days.

instance, feel discriminated against there will be grievances on which terrorism can feed, as it has among the Catholics in Northern Ireland.

Secondly, terrorists must as far as possible be dealt with under the existing law of the land. It is very easy for terrorists to claim that they are special people, who, because they are fighting for a political cause, should not be treated as criminals. The IRA, for instance, claimed that they were soldiers fighting the British government and should be treated as prisoners of war when captured, not as ordinary criminals. (In 1981 a number of IRA prisoners went on hunger strike to try to force the British government to accept this.) It is important, however, that society does not give terrorists a special status or importance but treats a terrorist killing as a murder, and thus an offence against criminal law like any other murder.

Most governments accept, however, that special powers are needed to deal with terrorism. In Britain there is the Prevention of Terrorism Act, which allows suspects to be held for up to seven days without trial (see below). As we saw on page 43 the British Government has also banned certain types of publicity for terrorist organizations. These laws certainly restrict human rights. The European Court of Human Rights has ruled that suspects should be brought before a court no longer than four days after arrest, compared to the seven days the British government allows.

When we consider how far such restrictions on human rights are justified we

FOCUS ON....

The Prevention of Terrorism Act

In October and November 1974 the IRA extended its campaign of terror to the British mainland. It launched a number of bomb attacks on pubs in Birmingham, Woolwich and Guildford. These attacks killed 28 people and injured over 250, many seriously.

The anger which these attacks aroused among the British public was intense. The police rounded up suspects and, while emotions were still high, these were tried and those found guilty were given long prison sentences. (Later, many were found to have been unfairly convicted and were released.)

The British government felt it had to respond to public anger and introduced the Prevention of Terrorism Act. This allowed police to detain suspected terrorists for, at first, two days and then a further five if the Home Secretary agreed. After that time they had to be charged or released. Under the same Act, there was the power to prevent suspects from moving between Northern Ireland and mainland Britain. The IRA and other terrorist organizations were also banned from operating in Britain. (Such organizations were already banned in Northern Ireland.)

The Act has now been extended to deal with international terrorism and those helping to finance terrorism. By preventing people travelling within their own country and by extending police powers of arrest, the Act does reduce human rights. The European Court of Human Rights has ruled against the Act on the grounds that any suspect has the right of a prompt appearance before a court, certainly in less than four days after arrest, let alone the seven allowed by the Act.

It has also been difficult to argue that the Act has been very successful. In the first nine months of 1988, 121 people were held under the Act but 99 of these were released without charge. Only 331 of the 5802 people held under the Act in its first nine-and-a-half years were later found guilty of an offence. The question is how many of these 331 could have been arrested and charged under other laws and how many cases of terrorism were actually prevented by the use of the Act.

need to look at the following questions. First, have the laws concerned actually increased the number of convicted terrorists or helped in other ways to reduce the use of terrorism? How far is it possible for outsiders to government to examine how the laws work in practice, or is the way they are imposed hidden in secrecy? Are they temporary laws which need to be renewed each year, or have they become part of the permanent law of a country (in which case they may be kept on as permanent restrictions, even after the terrorists have been defeated).

The reason why these questions are important is not only that these laws act as restrictions on human rights but that every new power a government takes on strengthens its position to take further powers. It has been a common practice in several parts of the world for governments claiming to be acting against terrorism to take on an ever widening selection of laws which are then used against the population as a whole. The main result of terrorism has thus become the destruction of democracy, not so much by the terrorists as by the government they are attacking.

There is no easy way to defeat a sustained campaign of terrorism against a democratic government. There is usually no alternative to calm and expert police work, so that terrorists can be detected, arrested and convicted under normal criminal laws, and to the continued determination of the government concerned to uphold a democratic way of life for all citizens, so far as the pressures of terrorism allow. There are few greater or more difficult challenges a democratic government can face.

THE FIGHT AGAINST INTERNATIONAL TERRORISM

As we saw in the case of the Kuwaiti hijacking (pages 3-4), an act of international terrorism can very quickly involve a number of governments. For international terrorism to be successfully controlled, there needs to be effective co-operation between governments. Three things are necessary if this is to happen.

First, there must be common international agreement as to what is meant by terrorism. It must be clear what acts of violence are to be treated as terrorist.

Secondly, it must be accepted that acts of international terrorism are attacks on the international community, not just the state immediately affected. It follows that all governments should accept a shared responsibility for dealing with acts of international terrorism.

Third, there must be some agreed way of bringing captured terrorists to justice. One view is that there should be an international law court to deal with such cases.

For combined action against terrorism we should look first at what the United Nations, which represents virtually every state in the world, has achieved. The United Nations first discussed terrorism in 1972.

For the Western nations things were fairly clear. They saw themselves as peaceful, democratic nations and they were outraged that terrorist violence should be used against them, their civilians and airliners. They were ready to support firm measures against terrorists.

On the other hand, many African and Asian nations had only become independent through the use of violence and they supported the struggles of other nationalist groups – in Southern Africa, for instance – to achieve freedom and independence. They were not prepared to allow acts of violence committed in the cause of liberation to be condemned as terrorism. As Mauritania, one of the African nations put it, 'the word terrorism could not be applied to persons who were denied the most elementary human rights, dignity and independence. Such peoples could not be blamed for committing desperate acts, which in themselves were reprehensible; rather the real culprits were those who were responsible for causing such desperation.' The representative for Madagascar put it another way claiming 'that acts of political terrorism undertaken to vindicate hallowed rights recognized by the

THE FIGHT AGAINST TERRORISM

FOCUS ON....

The United States and international terrorism

'We are attacked because of what we are and what we believe in.' So spoke George Shultz, the American Secretary of State, on the subject of terrorist attacks on the United States. In the 1980s the United States had become a major target for terrorists. According to American Government sources, between 1 January 1984 and 1 February 1985 there were 63 attacks on American diplomats and soldiers or their buildings. Forty-two people were killed in these attacks, 85 wounded and 3 kidnapped. In October 1984 there were over a hundred threats a week to American interests from different terrorist groups.

Why was the United States so vulnerable? First it is a superpower, the leading nation of the Western world – one whose economic and military interests seem to reach to every corner of the globe. Its wealth and the aggressive selling of the American way of life have been resented by many. Many Muslims, for instance, feel that Western values are a direct threat to their own.

At the same time, America has not been afraid to use her own military muscle. Her 'peacekeeping forces' in the Lebanon, for instance, used naval power to bomb Shia villages and one of her ships, the *USS Vincennes*, patrolling in the Persian Gulf in July 1988, shot down an Iranian airliner – believing it to be a hostile plane. Whatever the background to such incidents, they can easily be interpreted as acts of aggression and the object for revenge. By operating as a major military power in many parts of the world, the United States is bound to be seen as threatening to many.

In line with her power, American interests, embassies, military bases, banks and citizens are situated worldwide, thus making them very vulnerable to terrorist attack. As one Government spokesman put it: 'The basic problem is that we are out there in rather large numbers, so we are a relatively conspicuous target.'

There have been many bombings of American clubs and kidnappings of her citizens. The terrorist incidents which stand out include the massive bombing of the US Marines Headquarters in Beirut in October 1983, which, in effect, led to the withdrawal of American peacekeeping troops from the Lebanon. There was the hijacking of the TWA airliner in June 1985. In October 1985 the Italian cruise ship *Achille Lauro*, carrying many American passengers, was hijacked by Palestinians. They had been discovered on their way to launch an attack on Israel where the *Achille Lauro* was due to dock. One of these Americans, an elderly man in a wheelchair, was killed. In December 1988 there was the destruction by a bomb of another American airliner, over the Scottish town of Lockerbie.

The impact of these terrorist acts on the American public and government has been immense and the government has been under intense pressure to respond. In most cases there has been little it can do. It has had to learn the lesson that even the most powerful nation in the world is weak in the face of determined terrorism. Like most governments its response has varied. The USA withdrew from the Lebanon after the bomb attack there. It was ready to make argeements to have its hostages released after the TWA hijack in 1985, and was prepared to sell arms to Iran secretly in order to gain the release of American hostages held by pro-Iranian groups in the Lebanon.

In public, the US government has made a particularly determined public stand against states it accuses of sponsoring terrorism. Its list has included, at various times, Libya, Iran, Syria, Cuba, Nicaragua and the Soviet Union. In the early 1980s the view seemed to be that the Soviet Union was the power behind a network of states and groups prepared to use international terrorism. These charges were quietly

THE FIGHT AGAINST TERRORISM

dropped as relationships between the United States and the Soviet Union grew better in the mid-eighties. Syria was dropped from the 'list' when the Syrian government played a mediating role in gaining the release of the TWA hostages. With Iran the US government was in fact prepared to make deals behind the scenes. The main enemy remained Libya, particularly as her sponsorship of terrorism against American (and other) targets was open and unashamed.

It is not surprising that the United States felt frustrated by the continued attacks on her citizens sponsored by Libya. It felt that European nations, on whose territory many of the attacks took place, were not doing enough to combat them. In April 1986, American planes launched a bombing raid on Libya. Although the targets were supposed to be installations which could support the use of terrorism, civilians were inevitably killed. Despite all the distrust of Colonel Gadhaffi, such naked use of power caused a shockwave throughout the world with the British government, from whose territory the bombers flew, being one of the few publicly to support it.

It is true that the United States was under extreme pressure to take action – in particular from its own people. President Reagan's popularity reached its highest peak after the bombing. It is also true that many nations, both in East and West, were secretly pleased to see Gadhaffi being hit in this way. There is also some evidence that Gadhaffi acted in a more restrained way for some time after the raids. However, there remains concern that a massively armed superpower can act on its own in this way. Once civilians are killed, as they were in these raids, it is possible to argue that terrorism is simply being met by counter-terrorism.

United Nations were praiseworthy'. So there was not even agreement that acts of terrorism should be punished.

It took many years of discussion before in December 1985 the United Nations passed a resolution in its General Assembly that condemned without reservation 'as criminal, all acts, methods and practices of terrorism'. At the same time, however, it proclaimed the right of peoples to engage in armed struggle against colonial or racist governments. What some states may see as terrorism may thus be seen by others as violence used as a justified part of such a struggle. There is still no firm international agreement on what is actually meant by terrorism.

Resolutions of the United Nations do not require anyone actually to do anything. A better way of achieving action is a Convention. This is an agreement by which states promise to take action in certain cases. When there was a widespread outbreak of hijacking, for instance, a number of Conventions were drawn up. In the Hague Convention for the Suppression of the Unlawful Seizure of Aircraft of 1970 those who signed it agreed that captured hijackers should be sent to be tried either in the country where the hijacked plane was registered or in the country where it landed. If this was not done the country which had arrested the hijacker should try him or her. The next year the Montreal Convention extended this to cover acts of damage against aircraft, whether committed on the ground or in the air.

Conventions are not as strong as they may seem. Only those who sign them are bound by them. There is little that can be done to punish a state which signs a Convention and then fails to carry out what it has agreed to do.

The greatest progress has been made in Europe. The European Convention on the Suppression of Terrorism, drawn up in 1977, dealt with the issue of bringing terrorists who had committed a crime in

THE FIGHT AGAINST TERRORISM

one European state to justice in another. This removal from one state to another is called extradition. In the past a suspect who was wanted for a bomb attack committed, say, in Germany but who had fled to France could claim that the offence that the German government wished to try him for was committed for 'political' reasons. This was normally held to be a defence and the French government could refuse to extradite him.

Under the 1977 Convention it was agreed that a wide range of acts which were clearly terrorist, such as hijacking, taking hostages and exploding bombs, could no longer be claimed as political and thus the terrorist could be extradited to the country where the offence had been committed. Although the Convention only applies to Europe, it is the first step towards making the terrorist an international criminal, the enemy of all states, and dealt with by each state as such.

In April 1986 members of the European Community went further and made the first moves to deal with states supporting international terrorism. The American government had repeatedly asked them to be tougher on such states and had eventually taken the law into its own hands and bombed Libya – a state everyone agreed had been supporting international acts of terrorism. The European states realized that they needed to act more effectively, if only to prevent more bombing raids. They agreed to enforce stricter rules on the numbers and movements of diplomats from countries such as Libya and to ban the sale of all arms and other military equipment to states they pinpointed as sponsors of terrorism. They also agreed among themselves to co-operate more on intelligence operations against terrorism.

International co-operation against terrorism is still very limited. As we have seen, many states refuse to accept that certain acts of violence (those committed in the cause of 'national liberation') should be seen as terrorism. Even when there is agreement and Conventions have been signed it is difficult to ensure that each state acts as it has promised it would. In practice, under the pressure of events, many states are prepared to make their own deals with terrorist groups.

Which moves do you feel a democratic society should be able to use against terrorism?

1. Have powers to hold suspected terrorists without trial. For what period of time do you think this should be allowed?
2. Bring back the death penalty for all those convicted of terrorism.
3. Increase the number of surprise searches of homes in areas where terrorists are believed to be operating.
4. Increase the police force and be prepared to use the army to patrol streets.
5. Forbid interviews with terrorists in both newspapers and on television.
6. Increase the number of searches of people when they enter public places.
7. Anyone found carrying a weapon must prove that it is not being used to carry out an act of terrorism.
8. Police allowed to break up any meeting at which a supporter of the use of terrorism is speaking.

THE FIGHT AGAINST TERRORISM

9. Have the power to stop suspected terrorists moving from one part of the country to another.

10. Establish a secret police force with special powers to watch members of the public suspected of terrorism.

To answer these questions you need to be clear what you mean by a 'democratic' society (see text) and to consider carefully how far you believe the rights of all its citizens should be reduced in order to conduct a campaign against terrorism more effectively.

What do the comments of the Mauretanian and Madagascan governments quoted in this chapter tell you about the difficulties of coming to an agreed definition of terrorism?

What do you think are the best ways in which the international community can combine to fight terrorism?

7 Terrorism: A Conclusion

Terrorism has been compared to cancer. Cancer can strike a body at any time, in almost any part, and spread quickly from one part of the body to another. It can be difficult to control and can often end in death. Terrorism is much the same. As we have seen, terrorism can explode almost anywhere in the world and using modern communications and technology spread quickly to any part.

An important feature of terrorism is the way that each act of successful terrorism is quickly imitated by other groups. The hijacking of aircraft was first used in recent times by Palestinian groups but quickly spread all over the world, until effective methods were found to combat it. The kidnapping of hostages began in Latin America but then was widely used by terrorist groups in Europe, notably the Red Brigades in Italy. Car bombs were introduced by the IRA in their campaigns of the early 1970s. By the 1980s they were being successfully used in the Lebanon. The most recent technique is the planting of bombs timed to explode in an aircraft during flight. The Lockerbie disaster in December 1988 was the fourth 'successful' explosion of an aircraft in just over three years. The other three involved planes from India, Sri Lanka and South Korea.

This helps to show how difficult it is to control terrorism – but just how major a threat is terrorism to the peace of the world?

It is important to put terrorism in perspective. The United States government has estimated that between 1968 and 1974 there were 7435 terrorist incidents worldwide – killing a total of 4796 people. That is very similar to the number killed in one year on the roads of one American state, Texas. We should also compare these figures with the number killed in wars. There were an estimated million deaths in the conflict in Afghanistan between 1979 and 1989, for instance. Again, the Khmer Rouge government in Kampuchea is estimated to have killed some 300,000 of its opponents between 1975 and 1979. This makes terrorism appear to be a relatively minor problem.

This is not, of course, true, as the Chinese proverb 'Kill one, Frighten a thousand' reminds us. There may have been 'only' 4796 deaths, but the impact of these deaths has been immense. Look at the hijack of the TWA airliner in June 1985, for instance. One American citizen was killed, many others were put through a horrifying ordeal but did survive. Yet, at the time of the hijack, the world's most powerful state saw itself as facing a major international crisis, one which drove virtually every other piece of world and national news from its televison screens. This and other incidents caused major changes in the behaviour of American citizens, with hundreds of thousands changing their overseas travel plans. (In fact, those who did stay at home were more likely to die there from a road accident or murder than if they had travelled overseas.) There is no better example of the power of modern terrorism.

These deaths are important in another way. They represent a major threat to the democratic way of life and to the struggle to achieve human rights. As we have already said, terrorists are self-appointed, not elected. They attempt to bring about

TERRORISM: A CONCLUSION

change through violence and they are denying the human rights of those they kill or put at risk. So each death from terrorism represents an attack on ideals which many thousands, even millions, have achieved peacefully. So even though the number of deaths from international terrorism may appear small their impact and importance is far greater than the numbers suggest.

What does this imply for the future of the fight against terrorism? First, it is important to realize that it is unlikely that the use of terrorism will ever be completely prevented. It is impossible to keep control over the hundreds of groups or individuals who feel strongly enough about an issue or grievance for them to wish to use violence on its behalf. Terrorism is here to stay.

However, this should never stop us from looking at the situations where terrorism seems to flourish and to consider what long term measures might be used to stop it taking root. It would certainly be wrong to say that just because someone uses terrorism they must have a good cause. On the other hand, we must be aware of the kinds of frustration on which terrorism feeds and the possibilities of improving non-violent ways of expressing those frustrations.

Secondly, a great deal has been and can be done to prevent acts of terrorism. One is to maintain strict security procedures in areas which are especially vulnerable to attack. The most obvious are aircraft and here procedures have been tightened up enormously in the last 20 years. At the same time, there is room for a great deal of co-operation over intelligence on terrorist groups. In Europe this process is well under way through the so-called TREVI system of co-operation between governments and their police forces set up in the 1970s.

International co-operation against terrorism has, however, to take place at a far higher level than the pooling of intelligence information. As we saw in Chapter Six, it is important to see the terrorist as an enemy of all states, one which all governments are prepared to co-operate to eliminate. This means that governments must arrest terrorists of whatever nationality who land on their shores and either return them to the state where they committed terrorism or deal with them themselves. Some have even suggested an international court to deal with terrorists.

There are immense problems with any form of international co-operation, not only in that against terrorism. It was George Shultz, the United States Secretary of State in the final years of President Reagan's administration, who said 'We know the difference between terrorists and freedom fighters and our policies reflect that distinction'. He spoke as if the difference was an easy one to recognize – but clearly it is not. The Contras in Nicaragua were among those whom the Americans saw as 'freedom fighters', while to many their violence in so far as it involved the killing of civilians was terrorism. Is it possible to isolate specific kinds of violence, the hijacking of planes, the killing of unarmed civilians, the taking of hostages, for example and outlaw them irrespective of the ideal for which the group or individual carrying them out is fighting?

It is very difficult to track down and deal with a terrorist *group* who, after an act of terrorism, may melt away into their local community or disappear under the protection of a friendly state. It is easier for the international community to deal with a *state* sponsoring terrorism or offering protection to escaping terrorists. The European Community has agreed to stop arms sales to such a state and there are other economic sanctions. One proposal has been to ban all international flights to such a state as a protest against its support for terrorism. Few states can accept such isolation for long and such measures would certainly appear to be a more effective and justifiable response than violent retaliation.

The real challenge for a government

TERRORISM: A CONCLUSION

fighting terrorism, however, comes in the maintenance of democratic ideals when it is placed under immense strain by a campaign of terrorism operated against it. Every state under terrorist attack has felt compelled to take some extra powers, either through extending the force of the law or through using special armed groups. It has been argued, in fact, that the main result of terrorism has been to increase dictatorship.

As we have seen in our discussion of the British government's struggle against terrorism in Northern Ireland, it is very difficult to know where to draw the line fairly. The temptation is for a government facing a drawn-out and frustrating struggle against terrorism to introduce measures just to show that it is doing something. It could be said that the Prevention of Terrorism Act and the ban of interviews with the IRA and other terrorist organizations fall into this category. Do they actually reduce the use of terrorism? This would appear to be the question which needs to be kept at the forefront of debate on this issue.

Another temptation is to counter terrorism by the use of force. It is difficult to feel sympathy for a terrorist who is killed when he or she is actively preparing an act of terrorism. The use of violence against terrorists is usually immensely popular, as President Reagan found when he ordered the bombing of Libya. Thus governments are often tempted to use armed force in the fight against terrorism. It is all too easy for this use of force to escape democratic control or to break the international law on force, which only allows its use in self-defence. Action against terrorism can all too easily become counter-terrorism.

Governments must stand firm against terrorism. If they do not then certainly it will spread like a cancer which cannot be controlled. Terrorists can and will exploit weaknesses either in the will or the security arrangements of the states they attack.

The struggle will be a long drawn out one and will require much patience. It is possible, however, to isolate four different parts of a campaign against terrorism.

First effective co-operation through shared intelligence and good security arrangements is needed to prevent individual acts of terrorism before they happen. This may involve some temporary increase of government power.

Second, there needs to be agreed policy on how to deal with terrorist acts as they happen. This may involve a policy of no concessions to terrorists under any circumstances. It requires trained negotiators to deal with hostage-taking and armed groups such as the SAS which are able to resolve such situations when the hostages' lives are clearly threatened. Measures need to be worked out as how to best treat the world's press, who will invariably congregate around a terrorist incident.

Third, effective action has to be taken against captured terrorists. The aim should be to capture terrorists alive and special thought needs to be given as to how to do this without risk. Then the terrorist must be brought to trial. It is in this area where effective international co-operation is needed so that terrorists cannot find shelter.

Finally, international co-operation is needed against those states who sponsor terrorism. States do respond to being isolated in the world community but it needs a common will among the international community for this to happen.

There is no doubt that terrorism offers one of the most difficult challenges the international community has to face, but it is not the only one. Terrorism may have changed the lives of many millions of people in small ways but it has not destroyed human society. There are many other threats, from large scale war to government repression, from world hunger to environmental collapse which offer just as important challenges. It is important that the enormous publicity given to many acts of terrorism do not blind us to this fact.

Suggestions for further reading

WALTER LAQUEUR, *The Age of Terrorism*, Weidenfeld and Nicolson, 1986. This includes an historical background, details of a wide range of terrorist groups and also a section on terror as used by drug dealers. One of the fullest treatments of the subject overall.

STEPHEN SEGALLER, *Invisible Armies*, Michael Joseph, 1986. More immediately readable. It has a good chapter on the United States and terrorism and a full account of the *Achille Lauro* hijacking.

GRANT WARDLOW, *Political Terrorism*, Cambridge University Press, 198? More advanced reading. It looks in detail at the problems of defining terrorism and has a series of chapters on individual issues such as terrorism and publicity, the roles of the security forces in combating terrorism, etc.

PAUL WILKINSON, *Terrorism and the Liberal State*, Macmillan, 1977. Advanced reading but very good on the problems faced by democratic states in combating terrorism.

JULIET LODGE (editor), *The Threat of Terrorism*, Wheatsheaf, 1988. Provides a series of case studies on terrorism in Europe, including the IRA and Red Brigades, by recognized authorities.

The use of terrorism for purposes of publicity is covered well in ALEX SCHMID, *Violence as Communication*, Sage, London, 1982. CAROLINE MOORHEAD, *Fortune's Hostages*, Hamish Hamilton, 1980, although out of date and with nothing on hostage taking in the Lebanon, has good case studies of kidnapping in the 1970s.

The general problems involved in the use of violence are well dealt with in MICHAEL WALZER, *Just and Unjust Wars*, Pelican Books, 1980. Chapter Twelve deals specifically with terrorism.

The Baader-Meinhof Gang, one of the small revolutionary groups of the left, is analyzed in JILLIAN BECKER, *Hitler's Children*, Panther Books, 1978.

On Northern Ireland, a good introduction is PAUL ARTHUR and KEITH JEFFERY, *Northern Ireland since 1968*, Blackwells (for The Institute of Contemporary History), 1988.

DERVLA MURPHY, *A Place Apart*, Penguin, 1979 gives an excellent account of what it felt like to travel around Northern Ireland in the mid-1970s. It remains one of the best books written on the province. The best up-to-date history of the IRA is PATRICK BISHOP and EAMONN MALLIE, *The Provisional IRA*, Corgi Books, 1986. SALLY BELFRAGE, *The Crack, A Belfast Year*, Grafton Books, 1988, is also recommended. The controversy over the shoot-to-kill policy is well covered by the man who was sent to investigate it, JOHN STALKER, in his *Stalker*, Penguin Books, 1988.

There are many general books on the Middle East. See, for instance, HEATHER BLEANEY and RICHARD LAWLESS, *The Middle East since 1945*, Batsford, 1989. MAXIME RODINSON *Israel and the Arabs*, Pelican Books, 1982 is a more advanced treatment of the Arab-Israeli problem, but deals fully with the issues involved in the use of terrorism in the area. The best recent study of the Palestine Liberation Organization is HELENA COBBAN, *The Palestinian Liberation Organization, People, Power and Politics*, Cambridge University Press, 1984.

Glossary

Capitalism An economic system under which individuals with wealth are free to use that wealth with little restriction. It is assumed that they will seek profits. Capitalists argue that this form of society produces the greatest freedom and wealth for the community as a whole. Its opponents claim that it simply leads to greater inequality and the exploitation of the poor by the rich. In the 1970s, a number of European and Latin American groups used terrorism in an attempt to overthrow capitalist society.

Civilians Civilians are those who are not involved as combatants in a particular war or conflict, for instance, old people or children. Civilians have traditionally been given special protection at times of war but have often been the unintended victims of terrorism as passengers in aircraft or passers-by when a bomb explodes, for example.

Convention An agreement between a number of states; for instance, an agreement to act together in combating terrorism. For examples of Conventions dealing with terrorism, see Chapter 6.

Extradition The process by which a person who has committed an offence in one country but has escaped can be arrested in another country and returned to the country where the offence was committed. Recent conventions on terrorism are making it easier to deal with suspected terrorists in this way.

Democracy A system of government under which fundamental human rights are guaranteed and in which there is full participation by ordinary citizens in the process of government. Terrorism presents a major threat to democratic rule – see Chapter 6.

Fascism An authoritarian political system in which the nation or race is glorified above everything else. Fascists glorify conflict and war and fascism has thus often provided an inspiration for the use of terrorism by political groups of the right.

Guerrilla warfare Warfare conducted by small bands of armed men and women against a conventional army which could be that of their government or of an invader. Some but certainly not all guerrilla groups use terrorism as one of their tactics.

Hijacking The taking over of a plane, train, bus etc., by a group who intend to hold its passengers hostage. Normally threats are made to kill the hostages if the hijackers' demands are not met.

Hostages Hostages are those held prisoner by kidnappers or hijackers. Their lives are usually bargained with in the hope of achieving publicity, money or other political gains for the kidnappers.

International terrorism A term which covers a variety of terrorist acts with international effects, for instance attacks launched by a terrorist group in a foreign country, the co-operation of a number of terrorist groups from different countries, the hijackings of international flights and so on.

Media Newspapers, television and radio – in other words all the instruments of modern publicity. They can hardly ignore

GLOSSARY

acts of terrorism and so become used by terrorists as a means of gaining publicity. See Chapter 5.

National liberation movement An organization or group dedicated to seeking national freedom. This may be the removal of a foreign government (the IRA's campaign to free Ireland of British rule) or the setting up of a new state by breaking away from an old one (a Tamil state out of Sri Lanka, for instance).

Security forces Members of the army or police force concerned with combating terrorism or other unrest. Many states also have small highly trained groups (such as the SAS in Britain) who can carry out the rescuing of hostages or undercover work.

Shoot-to-kill policy A policy that known terrorists should be shot when discovered rather than being arrested and tried normally. There have been accusations that the security forces have operated a shoot-to-kill policy in Northern Ireland. (See Case Study on Northern Ireland, Chapter 3.)

State (a) A territory with fixed boundaries under a stable government (such as France or Britain); (b) The administration itself – its leaders, civil service, police and army.

State terrorism Terrorism used by a state as a means of controlling its citizens or destroying enemies.

Supergrass An informer. The term was used in Northern Ireland of those who provided information about terrorists to the security forces in return for not being charged for offences they may have committed. In practice, many super-grasses gave unreliable information and they are no longer widely used.

Terrorism Defined in this book as the use of, or threat of the use of, violence in order to achieve political ends. See Chapter 2.

Urban guerrilla A guerrilla (see guerrilla warfare) who carries out his campaign in a city. Because an urban guerrilla cannot easily isolate the forces of the government as he would in a remote rural area, he often uses terrorism against civilians as a major part of his campaign.

Index

Abu Nidal 14, 37
Achille Lauro hijack 54
Action Directe (France) 14, 17
African National Congress (ANC) 32
Al Jihad al-Islami (Islamic Holy War) 3, 38-9
Anti-semitism 18-19
Arafat, Yasser, 31, 32, 36, 47
Argentina 7, 13
ASALA (Armenian Secret Army) 10
Austria and terrorism 44

Baader-Meinhof Gang (West Germany) 14, 17
Black September 32, 41
Bloody Sunday (Northern Ireland) 21
British army, in Northern Ireland 20-29

Capitalism 16-17
Contra guerrillas (Nicaragua) 12, 59

Democracy and terrorism 48-9, 52-3, 58-60
Diplock Courts (Northern Ireland) 27

El Salvador 18
Enniskillen bombing (Northern Ireland) 4-5
ETA (Basque separatist movement) 10
European Community and terrorism 56
European Convention on the Suppression of Terrorism 55-6
Extradition 50

Fascism 18
Fateh (Palestinian Guerilla Group) 31, 33
Fateh Revolutionary Council 14, 37

Gadhaffi, Colonel 36-7
Gibraltar shootings 25, 28
Guardians of the Islamic Revolution 39
Guerrilla warfare 12-13

Guevara, Che 13

Hague Convention for the Suppression of the Unlawful Seizure of Aircraft 55
Hijacking 3-4, 32, 38, 50-1
Hizbollah (the Party of God) 38-9
Hostage taking 39, 50-1, 58

International terrorism 3-4, 8, 13-14, 53-7
Intifada 36
IRA (Irish Republican Army) 4-5, 14, 20-29
Iran 3, 38-9, 48
Iranian Embassy Seige 43, 51
Israel 30-37

Japanese United Red Army Group 14
Jordan 30, 32

Khomeini, Ayatollah 38-9
Kuwaiti aircraft hijack (1988) 3-4

Lebanon 9, 33-5
Libya, US bombing of 37, 55
Lockerbie air disaster 9, 46
Lod Airport Massacre 8, 14

Mao Zedong 12, 13
Media and terrorism 8, 41, 42
Montoneros 13
Montreal Convention 55
Moro, Aldo 16, 17, 44
Munich Olympics 41, 42

Nationalism and terrorism 10-11
Nazism 18
Northern Ireland 4-5, 20-29 (Case Study), 43, 46

Official IRA 21

Palestinians 9, 14, 15, 30-40 (Case Study), 41
PLO (Palestinian Liberation Organization) 31

Popular Front for the Liberation of Palestine 31-2
Prevention of Terrorism Act 52, 60
Provisional IRA 21 *See also* IRA
Publicity and terrorism 8, 41, 42

Racism 18-19
Red Brigades 14, 16-17, 44
Revolutionary terrorism 16-17
Royal Ulster Constabulary 26

SAS (Special Air Services) 25, 26-7, 28, 51
Satanic Verses 39
Semtex 8
Shi'ite terrorism 38-9
'Shoot to kill' 27-28
Sinn Fein (political wing of IRA) 25
Stalker inquiry 27
State sponsored terrorism 36-7, 54, 55, 59, 60
State terrorism 7
Supergrass 37

Tamils (in Sri Lanka) 11
Terrorism
  combatting terrorism 25-28, 48-57, 59-60
  definition of 6-15
  and democracy 48-9, 52-3
  effects of 41-7, 58
  explanations of 6-15
  strategies 41-7
Terrorists
  personalities of 9
  treatment of 27-8, 52, 59, 60
Tupermaros (Uruguay) 13, 17, 45-6

Ulster Defence Association 24
Ulster Defence Regiment 26
Ulster Volunteer Force 24
United Nations and terrorism 53, 55
United States and terrorism 39, 44, 45, 54-5, 58
Urban terrorism 13, 20-29
Uruguay 13, 17, 45-6

G.S.L. County, Sugar House ware Jan 31st 1856

My dear and affectionate Brother Joseph
it is with pleasure that I
set down to write a few lines to you to answer
your kind and ~~and~~ affectionate letter. I recieved it
this evning with the gratest of pleasure and
hapiness. ~~~~ to hear from you. John told me
that you was sick and I was sorry to hear
that for it will put you back a good deal I am
affraid but I hope ere this letter reaches you
you will be as well and harty as you ever was
thank the lord ~~for~~, that of helth is a blessing
that I enjoy I havnot been sick so as to be
confined to my bed a day sence you left home.
and I wish that it had been so with you but
the lord orders all things for the best. I hav
been going to school to 6 months now and am learning
midling fast and I intend to learn a good
deal faster than I have, we ~~have~~ got one of
the finest school houses in salt lake valley
and brother Eldredge keeps school and he is a
good school master. I hav got a dictionary and
I am sorry that I hav made mistakes in writing
to you and bothering you in reading my letters
but you must excuse me this time and I will try to
do better ~~this~~ time. thare is plenty of dictionary about and ~~~~ if you hav got a good one
I would advise you to keep it even if you cold
send it for I psume that it is an articu-